The Pain

The Pain and the Game is a retrospective look at the life of Damany Hendrix on his 35th birthday. His love for the game of basketball has caused him and his family much pain and grief. The game that he has loved so much has been a blessing and a curse. It has propelled him to emotional heights that he has yet to achieve off the court, and at the same time has caused him to feel the most pain he's ever felt in his young life. This is the story of a man who has loved a game to the detriment to his own development as a person. Now he's sacrificed so much for the game, he has lost so much that he has no choice but to give what he has left to the game that has taken much of his soul.

Intro: Happy Birthday to Me!

I am writing this in a hotel room by myself on my 35th birthday. My birthday has really made me take a retroactive look at my life. I decided to tell this story in hopes that my life can assist those that come behind me to be better prepared for the pitfalls that may loom ahead of them when it comes to the game we call life. Many of my stories are centered on basketball, but I feel like this story can assist people who have a passion for something in life. I hope you enjoy and thank you for reading. ,

Chapter 1: 2-7
"I am not afraid of the opinions of others-
but of being needed and coming up short"
John J. Geddes

The year was 1998. My high school, Vallejo Senior High, had become a powerhouse over the past two seasons and the Northern California Championship game was set to be the pinnacle moment for the high school athletically. We were a once in a generation type team. Our line up was loaded from top to bottom. We had two really good high school teams all on one roster. Our 12th man would have started on most high school teams. Our point guard Ty Johnson was a 5'10 freaky athletic football start that was also a really good basketball player. Ty was the only dude to ever dunk on me in high school other than my brother. He caught me slipping in an open gym. Ty would accept a scholarship offer from Arizona State to play football his senior year, but never got to go because of academic issues. He would play a few years of Junior College ball and play in the arena league once he completed his college career. Our other guard was Brandon Armstrong. Brandon was a 6'5 silky smooth guard who could do it all on offense. We had played together on varsity for the past three years and he had made himself into one of the top players in California. He would go on to forward spot they had McDonald's All-American, UCLA commit Ray Young. A 6'5 Super athletic dude, who was build like a grown man the moment he hit high school.

As the time ticked away, and the buzzer sounded, the tears fell from my eyes and I collapsed to the court, my life flashed before my eyes. I felt a weight drop upon my shoulders that pushed me deeper into the hardwood. At the age of seventeen I felt like this was the most pivotal moment of my life, and still believe it to this day. The Northern California final in 1998 was a highly anticipated game for the Bay Area. But for the city of Vallejo it was much more than that. The moment when that buzzer sounded, and I sat on the floor, tears pouring down my face, my teammate and childhood friend Darryl Walker comes over to me and says "get up, don't let 'em see you crying". I sat there, for a few seconds, he picked me up and I can't really remember much after that besides opposing players coming over to me and telling me "good game". It was all a blur, the next few hours became seconds, passing by like the landscape does as you peer out of the window of a car as a child. I don't remember Coach Wallace's post game speech, all I remember is my friend CC putting his arm around me on the way to the bus and telling me things would be ok. We lost the game by seven points after having the lead going into the fourth quarter. I went 2-7 from the field that night. As the leading scorer on the team, I needed to perform in order for us to win that game, and I hadn't. I had let my teammates down. What was even deeper than that, I felt like I let the city down. The year was 1998, and the game was the Northern California Championship game versus St. Joe's. St. Joes was a much storied program that had dominated the Northern California basketball scene for years. Along with a few other powerhouse programs. This was the school that Jason Kidd played for, and since he had gone there it was a hotbed for some great basketball teams. Little old Vallejo High was battling with one of NorCal's giants and going toe to toe. They had ended our season the year before in the NorCal Semifinals at Albany High outlasting us with a seven point win. They had also beaten us earlier that season in the De La Salle tournament. Yes, my last three high school losses were to the same damn team. Since then we had won twenty-eight straight. Had we won that game we would have faced Westchester high school out of LA for the State Championship. Obviously I was devastated, but I will end this on a funny note. As I sat on the bus, hat on, head down thinking about what I was going to do next, our teammate Mike Stewart was like a mother cow who had lost her baby bull, and would not stop talking and crying. He professed his love for all of us to the tune of about fifteen minutes before we had no choice but to laugh at this dude. It still brings a smile to my face when I think about it. Temporarily the pain would subside, but only for a short moment. We gathered that night, shared stories about the season, laughed, cried, and reflected.

After spending a few weeks walking around campus like my dog ran away, I was lucky enough to receive a scholarship offer from Gonzaga University. At the time, Gonzaga was a program on the rise, not the program that they are today. My brother had a very trying experience up there with the coaching staff and advised me not to go. As a seventeen year old kid I was pretty mature but not wise enough to really evaluate what was probably best for me. I wasn't ready for college on or off the court. In my life, school had always come easy to me as did mostly every aspect of my life, including basketball. I was naturally gifted at pretty much everything that I did. I was an All-star baseball player throughout little league and Babe Ruth. I was good at Pop Warner Football the one year that I played. That was the biggest part of my problem. As a young person when you have success at everything you never learn the value of having a great work ethic. I never learned good study habits, nor did I learn to push the limits athletically. It came to be a huge issue in my playing career, and as an adult. I have a hard time pushing myself to the limits.

My recruitment went very slow. I had a few local teams call me but no offers. That was when I learned that letters meant nothing. I had a shoe box full from Pepperdine, Gonzaga, USF, Santa Clara and a few more. I had a ton of media guides and literature from all of these schools, but only one offer from a school that my brother just did major work for. I will admit that I only got that offer because of him. I think he knew that but didn't want to hurt little bro's feelings so he advised me against taking it. My brother and I had an interesting relationship. He beat me up a lot when we were growing up, I guess this was his way of making me tougher, but as a kid you don't understand every lesson that people are trying to teach you. I didn't look up to him because he didn't really have early success when it came to the game of basketball. I can remember him being devastated after being cut from the Junior Varsity team as a freshman. He came home and sunk into his mattress as if he was trying to hide from the world. He shut his door and cried for hours. His passion for the game was insane. As a freshman, he was 5'8 with feet the size of a small giant. He got teased a lot and was always fighting at school. He got suspended so much but it's because he didn't take any lip from anyone. He fought because that was how he earned his respect. I have always respected him for that; whether he won a fight or lost he was never going to back down from anything or anyone. He took that same approach when it came to his basketball. I watched him fight through so much adversity and continuously prove people wrong. I admire that about him now and I wish I had some of that in me, but we are two different people. I watched him go from a guy who got cut from his JV team, to a guy who battled Joe Smith Toe to Toe at at open gym at Contra Costa Junior College in San Pablo. At the time, Chris Farr was the head coach and he used to hold these epic open gyms. Coach Farr was friends with J Kidd, Gary Payton, Joe Smith, Shareef Abdur-Rahim and other NBA players. At the time my brother was a Sophomore in College, and Joe Smith was a few years into the NBA. My brother is fearless. I mean this dude fears nothing in life. He got matched up against Joe Smith and I was scared for him. As I watched my brother battle and not give an inch to this NBA player I was proud. He gave Joe Smith the business on the offensive end and did a good job on him defensively. I had never thought that he was NBA level good, but that day I think he proved it to everyone, even himself. Getting back to the story, this was my first lesson about the game having no loyalty to anyone. This game could cause a ridiculous amount of pain and it has no prejudice. It did not care who you were, where you came from, or your economic status. It will break your heart, leave you at the altar, and move on to the next person while you watched. My brother's story has shaped my story a lot more than I realized until recently. We both have deep wounds when it comes to the game of basketball, but we have to keep grinding. His love for the game faded over time, while mine remained strong, mostly in the form of coaching, but in the end we both realize the damage it has done to us in our adult lives. Against his advice, I accepted the scholarship to Gonzaga and was headed to Spokane. Unknowingly unprepared.

Chapter 2: My Year at GU

As a freshman at Gonzaga, I dealt with plenty of ups and downs. Most of them stemmed from me not being prepared for college at any level. I thought because I was a good student at Vallejo High, and had an interest in math that I would major in computer science. I wish someone would have told me that you have to have a solid foundation in computer programming to take on this challenge. Needless to say I flunked that class and did not perform well my first semester. On top of my struggles in the classroom, I was the only one that didn't make the mile time of 5:45 so I had six am conditioning with the girls. I will say this about myself, I really need my lungs checked. We had a kid at Northridge that had lung issues. He was in good shape but would be gassed when we would run. We took him to get checked and turns out that he did have some problems with his lungs. They put him on some meds and he's never had issues since then. I truly believe that I have that same problem to this day. I could bust my butt and still feel like my lungs were going to explode. But I digress. I also pulled something in my pelvic area while I was in individual workouts trying to prove I didn't need to red-shirt. I had major struggles my first semester because I wasn't ready for college in any fashion. I would speak about being one of two African-American freshmen in the entire freshman class, and the only one in all of my classes but socially I was fine, I can adapt to any situation. I have always been a social butterfly and make a good situation in any instance. After accumulating a 0.8 GPA the first semester, I had to petition to take 21 units to make sure I completed the mandatory 24 in order to be eligible for my sophomore year. I passed all of my classes but in the midst of it all I had to cut back on my time in the gym. It probably seemed as if I was slacking but I was trying to make sure I could come back as a red-shirt freshman and play. This did not sit well with my coaches. The funny thing is that I was stronger than I had ever been, in the best shape of my life and more athletic than I had ever been. This was the only time in my life that I could 360 in either direction off of two feet. For a one leg jumper that was a huge accomplishment for me. In the midst of all of my messing up, the team makes an amazing Cinderella run to the Elite 8 becoming America's darling. In the first round we were matched up against Minnesota and we were able to pull off the first of 3 upsets. In the next round we got to play Stanford who was a 2 seed and one of the favorites to make it to the final four because they had returned many of the players from the year before in which they had made it to the Final Four. Watching from the bench with my young basketball eyes, it seemed to me that Stanford was not prepared for that game. Basketball at that level is all about preparation.. Here is what I think happened. In a tournament setting you anticipate who you might play in the second round and you acquire film on both opponents. As a staff the coaches at Stanford may have overlooked us and been preparing to play Minnesota. I am sure they got some film, and watched the Minnesota game trying to prepare, but it was evident to me that they didn't do a great job. I just remember them running into so many screens and being late chasing our guys around the perimeter. We end up beating Stanford and that was when the media started to take a notice. Going into the sweet 16 the tournament ratchets up about three notches. Now on the way to the arena you have a police escort from your hotel to the arena. The media coverages is probably double what it was in the first two rounds. Your food starts to taste a little better and the sky is a bit brighter. This was my second experience on the road because I didn't travel with the team during school because of my academic issues. The coaches wanted us to be a part of the experience and I am grateful to have gotten a chance to see these things. We were matched up against Florida in the next round. Florida was really talented but also very young. Two of their better players were Mike Miller, long time NBA vet, Udonis Haslem, another long time NBA vet and Teddy Dupay. They were really good but all Freshman. They played us tough and had a one point lead down the stretch. I cannot remember the play by as the time got under three seconds, a shot went up, bounced around on the rim and Casey Calvary tipped it in for us and we won the game and were going to the Elite 8. We stormed the court, Casey was tackled by the entire team and sports illustrated got a great picture and we were now Americas Darlings. In the next round we would lose to the eventual National Champs the UCONN Huskies, who were led by Richard "Rip" Hamilton and Khalid El-Amin. It was such a crazy ride, that I was able to witness with my own eyes. I felt like my hard work was paying off and I was going to be an important part of the program's future. I was really excited about next year and the prospect of being a guy that was on the court during these moments instead of being in street clothes. After the season I began to hear whispers about me not being a part of the program the following year. The graduate assistant coach at the time, Scott Snyder, used to hang out with the players as he was a recent graduate. He would tell the guys the things the coaches would say about me and another freshman that was red-shirting with me, my boy Eric Chilton. Eric was 7'2 and if I could imagine what the character "Lurch" would look like as a human being, I think Chilly was it. He didn't even really like basketball but played solely because he was tall. His brother was a stud at Colorado State. He had no love for the game and really had a rough time at GU. He and I were really close that year and we could lean on each other when necessary. Chilly was a really cool guy and he and I became really good friends. Scott Snider would tell the players that the coaching staff was thinking of not bringing Chilly back the following year, and that they were on the fence about me.

One morning we had a jog-a-thon and I decided not to attend. I don't know why I didn't go, but it proved to be a really bad decision. It seems as if this was the straw the broke the camel's back. A few days later I was called into the office and was told that the coaches had decided not to renew my scholarship. Many players think that an athletic scholarship is a five year contract to play four years of your respective sport. That is not the case. Athletic scholarships are for one year, and if the school chooses not to renew you scholarship they are well within their rights. As an eighteen year old kid, how do you deal with losing a scholarship? My face not flinching, in my not wanting to show them how much pain they were causing me, the tears poured down my face like a faucet that would never quite turn off. I didn't say much, I left the office and wandered the campus for who knows how long. Lost in my thoughts, and emotions, I wandered like a nomad traversing through terrains never explored by man. I remember I had on a Cleveland Indians hat. I pulled it down and began walking with no destination. I had no idea what to do. I had no idea who to talk to. What was I going to tell my parents? What would they think? What would my friends think? What would Vallejo think? Many athletes before me that had received scholarships had returned home for numerous reasons. Some were kicked out of their schools for their conduct, others had chosen different paths in life, and some had just washed out. Now, I would be another Vallejo athlete who couldn't make it. My world had come crashing down. I was always a very naive young man. I thought people were intrinsically good like I was. I am not saying that the coaches aren't good people, because I know them in my adulthood and I have a relationship with all three of them and they are solid guys. I have learned so much about the business that I can't harbor any hard feelings towards them. I wasn't handling my business like I should have been, so they thought it would be best to use my scholarship elsewhere. Are there times that I think that I got a raw deal? Sure, but I know the business now so I don't blame them for terminating my scholarship.

Eventually, I returned to my room and sat down to collect my thoughts. After a few minutes my boy Quentin Hall, more affectionately known as Q, came and knocked on my window for me to let him in. Q and I had become pretty tight. Q was an all heart point guard from the Bahamas and was the heart and soul of that team. He's all of 5'8 and I saw him lock up Arthur Lee, All-American point guard from Stanford in a win, Quincy Lewis, a 6'8 wing that led the country in scoring that year from the University of Minnesota, and Florida's Guards, and Khalid El-Amin of UCONN, all in the run to the Elite 8. This is my dude to this day. He sees my eyes are bloodshot red and asks me "What's wrong?" I told him the coaches had taken my scholarship away and he was furious. He storms off towards the office as if to defend a younger sibling that had been being picked on, but they didn't really talk to him. In the mean time I had to tell my family that I just lost my scholarship and I had to come home. How do you tell your people that? I called my brother first for some reason, and to my surprise he was on the first thing smoking. My parents never came up to Spokane to defend me, but big bro came out and had it out with the coaches. I didn't speak to the coaching staff before leaving; I went back to California and tried to put the pieces back together. At eighteen, I was back home, with no school, heartbroken by the game that I loved so much. Why did this have to happen to me? I had no time to be hurt, I had to find a new situation because my father was very unhappy with me and I knew once I returned home that I had to have a plan. For years, this would put a small fracture in our relationship. We still have never spoken of it, but I know he was disappointed in me, and I too was disappointed. I was disappointed that he didn't have my back and come fight for me like he had done for my brother when he was going through his struggles. Why was his situation any different from mine? Why did he have his back and not mine? These are the questions that you ask at eighteen and your whole world has come crumbling down around you and all commodities and that the moment that you couldn't do something for the coach is the moment you became expendable. You're essentially a worker, a commodity to do the goods of the institution that you compete for. Collegiate basketball players are nothing more than pieces to help the coach achieve their success and climb the ladder. College sports are not about the players. It's about the governing bodies and the institutions. I wouldn't say that its exploitation, but collegiate athletics is becoming less about the athlete. This year was a very emotional year for me. I was still fragile from what had just happened to me and I am sure the coach knew this, and would use this in order to get me to conform. He was a verbally abusive coach who had no regard for rules, and because of that we were on probation and could not compete in the playoffs. This was another piece of information that I should have heard about while on my visit at some point. I could tell a number of stories about this season but I will only tell the best ones. This man was a cold hearted and callous a human being that I have ever come across. If you looked into his face it was devoid of compassion, lifeless and empty, as if he had no soul. He cut two returners who played major minutes for a really good team the previous year. One young man was from Milwaukee Wisconsin, and was the backup PG who felt like he would be a starter this season. I thought He was a really good player, but coming into the junior college was a really good local point guard. He didn't even allow the kid from Milwaukee to try out for the team to make room for this local kid. Now he's got this young man thousands of miles away from home and he's not even playing basketball which is why he came in the first place. I saw some things that summer that made my stomach turn when I think about them. He would fly guys in for an open gym, let them play for a game or two, if they weren't good he wouldn't allow them back on the court and then send them home on a greyhound bus. At the time I was nineteen, going into my sophomore year and I felt really bad for these young men that just wanted to play ball. It was the coldest thing I had ever seen at the time.

That team was one of the most talented and together teams that I had ever played on. The reason we were so tight is because we all knew we had a crazy coach that got off on tormenting us. It made us play for each other and for the most part we had a very successful season. Unfortunately because of some of his recruiting transgressions, we were ineligible and could not compete in the post season. This was a very emotional year for me because of what I had just gone through. This particular coach would constantly make reference to the fact that GU had "sent my ass home". He knew he could go there to break me down, and unfortunately I was not equipped with the tools to deal with those moments. His whole deal was that he wanted us to "submit" to him and his ways. This is a common thing among coaches but most are tactful about getting their players to "buy in" or "submit". Not this coach. He would flat out tell us to "submit". I will share this particular story in hopes that it will frame his mindset as a coach, take from it what you will.

After a game one evening, during our post game talk, a game that we won by the way, Coach goes bananas. We were at Contra Costa College who didn't win a game all year. During this speech the coach says to us "you're all my bitches, I mean in the terms that you guys use it these days, you're all my bitches". Then he starts talking about how he tells us what to do, and we have no choice, to try to take the sting out of calling us bitches, but still emphasizing that he is fully in charge and there is nothing any of us can do about it. As I look back, he really had a master/slave mentality. I remember my teammates and I looking around in extreme disbelief, and confusion. We were offended, but didn't really know what to do. No one said a word. After we got home, some of my teammates and I talked about what had just happened and we were enraged, but as kids we didn't know what to do. Many times as an athlete you just want to play, and you don't want to do anything to jeopardize that. I think that's where we were with that whole speech, so we let it go.

Going into the year, I wanted to make sure I got my Associates degree so I could transfer after my first year. I had a solid year but I didn't get any offers. I thought I was one of the better players in the state, and I didn't understand the lack of attention I was getting in terms of recruiting. I have another story to let you know the struggles of that year. We played a game and won. I guess Coach didn't like the fact that we missed a ton of charge opportunities. He scheduled a practice at 6 am the next day. We stumble into practice half sleep, bodies sore from the previous night's game, and we were taking charges for almost two hours. For those that don't know what a charge is, is when an offensive player is driving and you step in front of him or her and they knock you to the floor in order to draw an offensive foul on the player with the ball. We were literally in groups of three, taking charges from our teammates for hours. Thank god it was a school day or I think we would have been taking charges until he got tired of watching us. Before we left practice he tells us to be back at 4pm for another practice. This is all on a game day. We come back for another two-hour practice before our game at 7:30 that evening. As we sit in the locker room, beaten and tired like quarter horses preparing for a race, Coach walks in and goes over the game keys and scouting report. Prior to him sending us out to warm up he tells us, "I don't care that you guys had two practices today. If you don't win this game by fifty we are going to practice right after the game." That night we were playing Pacific Union College, whom I never heard of before, but needless to say we figured we would be practicing after the game. It is not realistic to think you can beat a team by fifty points at the college level. To this day that is still the biggest margin of victory that I have ever been a part of; we ended up winning by fifty-one points. I don't think he thought we would win that game by fifty points, but he did know that we would win the game easily which is why I am sure he had us practice twice on that day, but that was still an insane way to challenge your team. The second day of back to back, you practice twice on the day of the second game and tell your team they had better win by fifty. He made us do a lot of improbable things just so he could come down on us and make us "submit". As I have grown into being a coach with his own philosophy I thought he did an awful job working with young athletes. I am not saying that because he was hard on us, or verbally abusive, I just feel like he had to assert his dominance over us daily, and I really feel like he didn't care about any of us as people. It was evident to me that we were just pawns to him. We were only there to win games for him. To dribble for him, pass for him, shoot for him. We were empty shells there to carry out his plans, to achieve his goals, for his victory. In my opinion, if you are going to be authoritarian you have to care about your kids. Kids will play their hearts out for a coach that cares even if he is extremely tough on them. There has to be an element of love there or it won't work well in most cases. We won because we were talented not because he did a great job.

When the season ended and I had no scholarship offers and I began to hear that he was saying things about me to coaches that would turn them off from recruiting me. He was saying that I was un-coachable, not a winner, lazy and anything he could possibly say to get them to not recruit me. One day I went into his office and left him a list of Historically Black Colleges to call because I just wanted to go somewhere and play ball and enjoy my college experience. I received my Associates degree so I was qualified to transfer to any of the school on the list and receive a full scholarship. He called me in the office and pretty much said he wasn't going to call them for me and that if I stayed another year I could play my way into a really good situation. He was a master manipulator, and again I was a very quiet kid who didn't speak up for himself so I let him get into my head. He played my little mind like a fiddle, strumming strings, and playing the chords of my life, until we were playing the same song. Though I was quiet, I had the intelligence enough to know that I had to get out of the situation, so I began looking for another Junior College to transfer to. A few weeks after the season ended the Coach was fired for his recruiting violations. This let me further know that I had to get out of there as soon as possible. I visited the Junior College closest to my home of Vallejo which is

Solano Community College. I was prepared to take 12 summer units to ensure that I could be eligible for the entire upcoming season. When I met with the coach at the time, Jerry Miller, I asked what type of help he would give me so that I could receive a scholarship when the season was over. He told my brother and me that he doesn't make phone calls for players and college coaches will find players if they are good enough. I was young but I had been around enough to know that coaches were not knocking down the doors at SCC to see their kids. Around that same time, Coach Brett Paige, who was an assistant at Santa Rosa gave me a call about the Coach that they had hired. I told him that I was planning on leaving and that I had been visiting different schools. Coach Paige said to me that "You're going to be our best player, I have talked to Coach McMillan about you and he wants you to come back". I set up a meeting with Coach McMillan and sat down with him. This meeting was the first time that I had heard how the previous coach was dogging me. The previous coach told him that he should get rid of me, that I was the worst of the worst, I was un-coachable and he couldn't win with me. I was so in shock because he and I had never had any type of altercation. I never talked back to adults in positions of authority. That was something that my parents really instilled in me as a young man. I let that man verbally abuse me for an entire season and for him to say that to me was beyond my comprehension. Coach McMillan was a local legend from Cloverdale High School. He was an All-American High school player, a four year starter at the University of Arizona and went to the final four with Sean Elliott, Steve Kerr, and Tom Tolbert. Coach Mac sat me down, told me everything the previous coach had told him about me, and the good things the Coach Paige had told him about me. Coach Paige had known me since I was 15 years old. My AAU team played against his program for several years. He was part of the reason I went to Santa Rosa. He vouched for my character and me as a player which canceled out what the previous coach said. Coach Mac agreed to give me a clean slate and he would only judge me from the things that I showed him. I felt like that was fair enough and I decided to go back to SRJC. It was that moment that Coach Mac literally saved my career. Many people don't know this but I was ready to hang up my basketball shoes. This is why I am still loyal to Coach Mac to this day; I don't think that he knows how close I was to being done playing the game.

Chapter 4: Year 2 at SRJC
"Our greatest glory is not in never falling, but in rising every tine we fall'"
Confucius

My second year at Santa Rosa was the best year of my career. The team was successful; we reached number 2 in the state of California and stayed there for the majority of the year. Because I had graduated the previous semester I had a light load the first to start the year. I was taking a few online classes and I only had to attend class on Friday afternoons. Saturday through Thursday I could spend time in the gym because I didn't have anything else that I was obligated to do. In short, I probably had the best year in SRJC history. I was top 10 in the state in Points at almost 23 per game, rebounds (10.1), field goal percentage (above 60), 3 point percentage (roughly 48) and free throw percentage (over 90). You would have been hard pressed to find stats that matched mine that year. I was an All-State selection, Conference MVP, I even had a triple double that year at Mendocino, and the stat line was stat line was 32 points, 13 boards and 10 assists. It was one of those games that I was just working and after the game the stat person pointed it out to me. I had plenty of games that year where I would have close to 30 and not even realize it. I used to watch this video tape I had of Michael Jordan and the Bulls vs. the Knicks. The famous double nickel game where he just destroyed them. That's when I started to watch the game from a different lens. I watched the offensive action. The way he got to his spots. NBA players predominantly shoot from the same spots on the floor. Those are the shots that they work on the most. Mike was surgical in the pinch post, the elbow area. I really worked on my long post game that year and that was my go to. Most times I would just face up and shoot the short jump shot over my defender with a little fade on my shot. I was being heavily recruited, but I wasn't getting the attention from any high major school. There were no Pac-10 schools showing any interest. I did get some literature from Northwestern, but I doubt that I could have gotten in. They have a pretty rigorous entrance process and although I had made the presidents list that first semester I still had a long way to go to make up for that freshman year. I really wasn't interested in making up for it. I still wonder why I never received much interest from the Pac. I was receiving a lot of attention from the Big Sky, Big West, and a few schools in the WCC. All was well, we were 28-3, we finished 13-1 in league, we had won 22 games in a row at one point and we were riding high.

My recruiting was picking up; I was up to about 10 scholarship offers, many from the Pacific Northwest area. The Idaho schools had all offered me as well as the Montana Schools. My parents were not really involved in my process; they allowed me to make my own decision coming out of high school and this time around as well. This may have been an issue looking back because I made some interesting decisions. I declined all of the school in the Pacific Northwest simply because they were in Gonzaga's region of the United States. I didn't want to deal with the weather, and wanted to go to a school with a bit more diversity. When you are choosing a school to play basketball these are factors only if basketball is a piece of what you want to get out of your college experience. At this point, I wanted to enjoy the last few years of my college experience. A small school in Texas called Lamar University started recruiting me very heavily. I knew nothing about their program so I didn't really take them too seriously. Long Beach State was interested but never offered me a scholarship. If I can remember correctly that is where I would have liked to go since no Pac-12 schools were showing any interest in me. Coach Ernie Kent and the University of Oregon were recruiting my teammate Robert Johnson very heavily. At the time Oregon was really good and I would have loved to go there. Coach Kent came to practice one day, and most days Rob and I were matched up against one another. That year, Robert was also an All-State selection and led the state in rebounds and blocked shots. We were pretty much the only ones who could compete against one another so most days coach put us up against each other. I was a pure scorer and Rob was an all around really good basketball player. He was a great defender, rebounder and passer. He had a high IQ and was the center piece of our team. Although I made our offense work, he was the most important piece to the team. He defended the rim and we could run our offense through him because he was a great decision maker. The day that Coach Kent came to practice I had decided to destroy Rob. As good of a defender as he was he could not guard me. I doubt that there was anyone in the California Junior College system that could guard me that year. I was a third year bounce back who could shoot the three, go off the bounce, shoot the mid range off the bounce, score in the mid post, pinch post and on the block. I was pretty unfair. So I absolutely destroyed Rob that day in practice. I figure if he came to watch Rob, and I killed the guy he came to see that he would take notice and want to take a closer look at me. I didn't understand the dynamics of "need". They didn't need another with scorer. They had two pros on their wings in Luke Jackson and Fredrick Jones. I could have cooked Rob until the cows came home and it wouldn't have mattered. I didn't understand it then but I get it now. He did call me in the office and say he was impressed and that he liked my game. I do have to say this about Rob though. I feel like I am I am not giving him his due. Robert Johnson probably has the nastiest dunk on me of my career. I have met some folks are the rim, I was a sneaky good shot blocker, ask Casey Calvary and Kelvin Torbert. One day in zig zag drill, Rob and I are battling as we normally did, I came down and hit him with a wiggle move and popped a pull up on him. He came down and I will never forget this. We were to the left of the top of the key, Rob has the ball in his right hand and he hit me with a between the legs cross over and brought it back through his legs back to his right hand and took off. He had a good step and a half on me and I tried to catch up. He rose up and I tried to get him and he crammed that thing on me something ridiculous. It was so bad I couldn't even get mad; I had to give him his props. All the buckets I scored on Rob those two years at the JC together will never make up for that one bang out!

I didn't end up going to Oregon but Rob did. I believe they made an Elite 8 run his senior year with Luke Ridnour and Luke Jackson and company. My recruiting had been narrowed down to Loyola Marymount, Sac State and surprisingly Lamar. LMU wanted me to play the 4/3 and I knew I was a bit undersized to play the 4 in the WCC. I was wrapped up in the position that I was going to play vs. the things that really mattered. I would have been a complete mismatch at the 4 in the league. I wasn't advanced enough in my basketball thinking to understand that at the time. When I went on my visit I really didn't feel welcome by the team either. Rob and I actually went on this visit together. He had Oregon in his pocket and told me the only way he would think about going there is if I went. We would have been really good together in that league. The guys just didn't seem to vibe with us. I know now that the majority of the guys were from LA, and having lived there I now understand how they are as people. As a 20 year old kid I wasn't really aware, I felt like they didn't want us there. Our hosts didn't even play our positions. I had some friends from high school that we randomly ran into on our visit, so I stopped to hang out with them and catch up. It's funny because the friends were actually on the cheerleading squad when we were in high school. I remember to this day my friend Tinetta was sick and wouldn't come out of her room. So we hung out for a few and in the midst of it all our hosts left us with them. It was no big deal, but it did stick with me and reaffirm my thoughts about them. I wanted my last two years to be enjoyable, and I didn't feel like LMU would be a good "home" for me. If I had it to do over again I would have chosen LMU for two reasons. Location would have been the primary reason. If I would have been thinking about my future after basketball, LMU would have set me up really nice. I am sure I would have been able to build a network of people, and future employment opportunities. I also would have picked LMU for the chance to play GU four times in two years if not more. Revenge wasn't high on my priority list. As I look back maybe it should have been. I don't feel like I made the wrong choice not choosing LMU, but I can look back at see that it probably would have been very beneficial to my future, and who wouldn't want to go to school in So Cal on that beautiful campus? But I chose against it.

I also took a trip to Sac State. I don't even think my parents knew I took an official visit there. I drove up there by myself and did the tour thing, and had a good time. I had a good rapport with the coaching staff; Coach Jenkins was a cool young black coach that players could vibe with. Sac State was a program that had been very bad for a long time. They needed a guy, and they wanted me to be that guy. It was important to me that I'd be the number 1 option offensively. This decision was 90% based on if the offense would run through me. That's who I was as a player. I scored the ball. I wanted to go to a school that was going to give me the ball. That's also a big reason why I didn't choose to go to LMU. They liked me and they wanted me to be a "part" of their offense, but I needed to be the focal point. Not to say that had I gone to LMU that I couldn't have played my way into the lead role like I had on every team I had played on prior to, but there's a different comfort when you have a coach tell you that that wants you to be the guy. Coach Jenkins was telling me that he wanted me to be that guy. So I took a serious look at Sac State. My host on the trip was Rene Jacques. Rene was a guard for St. Joes, how ironic was that? I had a hatred for St. Joes that still runs pretty deep. The last three losses of my high school career came at the hands of Joes. They beat us in the Nor Cal semi finals my junior year ending our season, they beat us in the De La Salle tournament early in my senior year, and after a 28 game win streak, they beat us in the Nor Cal Finals. So you can see why I didn't too much care for anyone that went to St. Joes. But Rene and I were cool, and kicked it on the recruiting trip. The coaches got me tickets to see DL Hughley, that was pretty cool. We didn't stay long though. We went to a party or something. The trip to Sac State was cool, but I think I didn't go there because of the reputation of the school. If you were from Northern California you didn't go play ball there if you had other options. Not that LMU or Lamar had much better reputations at the time but the stigma was bad about Sac State.

Needless to say I didn't sign with Sac State. Lamar was putting on the full court press. I didn't know anything about the school at all but the coaching staff was doing a really good job of recruiting me. I liked the fact that it was in Texas and not too far from Houston. Lamar is located in Beaumont, Texas. At the time the population was about 112,000 people. It was the first city in Texas where oil was found. I used to spend my summers in Houston when I was younger. My parents would send my brother and me to stay with her cousin. I loved Houston and I had a bunch of family that lived there. It was almost like a second home. While I was on my visit I really felt a connection with the players. I had been on several recruiting trips by this time in my life so the wooing wasn't a big deal. I was more worried about fit and enjoying the experience. There is nothing like playing with a group of guys that you get along with. The fellas seemed very close and they really embraced me. They were really excited about me coming, like I was the missing piece to them being a good team. I felt an instant connection with the guys. I left that trip with a really good feeling about Lamar. They had a beautiful arena, nice facilities and Beaumont wasn't a bad place to me. I could do two years there. The coaching staff clearly stated that they wanted me to come a score, a lot. They assured that I would be the number one option offensively. My mindset when I left SRJC was to lead the country in scoring. I felt like this was a place that I could do that. I didn't commit before I left, but I pretty much knew where I would be spending my next two years of college.

After I returned home I sat down with my parents and told them I thought Lamar would be a good situation for me. We had very little communication about my choice up to that point. But I told them I liked the school, the coaching staff and the players.

Mike Deane was the Head coach at the time. Mike was a very charismatic and charming coach. Mike was an old school coach who grew up in New York and was a straight shooter. With over 400 career wins, his resume spoke for itself. Mike was a great coach but would turn into a lunatic when the lights were on. He was a yeller/screamer and at times was very hard to play for. Of course none of the players told me this while we were on our trip once again. As the time winded down on signing day, it was still between LMU and Lamar. Mike, and we called him Mike because he wouldn't let us call him Coach Deane, flew out from Texas, sat with my parents and me for about an hour and told me that he wanted me to SHOOT THE BALL. He was very impressed with me as a scorer and wanted to use all of my talents offensively. He said I could run the trail spot; he would use me in the post, and allow me total freedom to do my thing offensively. I had one question for him, where do I sign? Mike flew in and out in the same day and that was impressive to me. So on signing day, by myself, I signed my letter of intent to Lamar University, took it to the AD's office got a copy made, and mailed it off. I was officially a Lamar Cardinal.

This was a proud moment for me because just months earlier I was close to giving up the game of basketball. I had overcome a lot to get to that point and still to the day I am proud of the day I signed my second NLI. I had earned that scholarship through my play and that was it. I became one of the best players in California and was now going to take my talents to the Southland Conference. I finally felt like things were looking up. I felt for the first time that the game was on my side. There was a devastating ending to our season but I was on my way to a situation that I thought would be great. I finally felt like things were looking up and the game would not continue to betray me and my happiness.

Chapter 5: LU baby
*"Challenges are what makes life interesting
and overcoming them is what makes life meaningful."*

Things were looking up. I felt like this move would make up for all of the pain and strife I had gone through. I was going to be the man and enjoy the final two years of my college experience. For the most part that was true but these next two years would have plenty of pitfalls that awaited me. I was the first of my teammates to hit campus. The coaches came and picked me up, got me moved in and got me situated. Shortly after I got there, my guy Hayes Grooms IV and his family came in. Hayes was an incoming freshman from Brother Rice High School in Detroit. He was 6'1 and slim, as most eighteen year old kids are. His mother and father came with him and I got to meet the family. They were very nice people and really cared for Hayes. Hayes was a nice kid that came from good stalk. He and I had to come in early in order to take the TASP test. It was an entrance exam that tested your math and English skills. Every student has to take in when you go to school in the state of Texas. It may be for state schools only but either way I had to take it. It didn't make any sense to me because I had an Associate's degree but whatever. So Hayes and I chopped it up for the days that we were there and were really cool. Hayes and I are still really good friends. He eventually transferred to Michigan and graduated a Wolverine.

As the other players rolled into town and got settled in, we started having some open gyms. The parents were still around and were invited to the open gyms to watch. Since we had everyone in the gym I felt like I needed to assert my position on the team as the "guy". When I tell you that these three days may have been the best stretch of shot making I have ever put together, you had better believe it. I destroyed anybody and everybody that was in my vicinity. I was on a mission and after the dust settled it was clear who the big dog in the gym was. I was pulling from two steps across half court and banging 3's, I was getting to the rack, and I was taking dudes to the block. I impressed myself. My objective was accomplished after those three days. I had parents coming up to me afterwards saying how they liked watching me play, and how they were impressed with me. It was a good feeling. My teammates and I still meet up when one of us gets married or when we can put together a trip, and we still talk about those three days. Hayes has told me the things his dad said about those open gyms. It was truly a legendary experience. The third day I wasn't as hot as I had been from the perimeter the previous two days and Mike wanted to meet with me to work on my shot preparation. He said I had the best hands he had ever coached. He was referring to my shot once I got into it, but wanted me to work on getting the ball "ready" to be shot. I struggled with this for the next two years and never really shot it as well as I had after leaving GU. I became a good shooter in Spokane because I spent 2 hours a day pretty much getting shots up while the guys practiced. For the two years I spent at Santa Rosa I shot in the mid 40's from 3. I never cracked 40% again after that. I am not saying that what they did hurt my shot but I was never consistent after that.

Soon after, school started and we got into our preseason condition program and our weight program. Mike wasn't huge on running us silly, but we did a fair amount of conditioning. I was always a guy that needed to be pushed to my max because I didn't have the internal drive to get myself in shape. That was by biggest deterrent when it came to reaching my full potential, which I never did. I hated running, and still do to this day. I swear there is something wrong with my lungs. Even when I was in mid season shape I would be so tired. I swear there is something wrong with me. I learned to play tired but most times I was pacing myself, and as we all know, you can't pace yourself at the college level. Luckily for me I was always one of the more skilled players on the court offensively. Mike preserved our bodies well. He was a technician of a coach, a big X and O guy. He was a wealth of knowledge that I learned a lot from. He was also a yeller/screamer. Mike was a 6'1 former PG from New York. He used to tell us they used to call him "White Mike". He would tell us his stories of playing on the playground with the "brothers". Mike was a genuinely nice guy who really cared for us off the court. On the flip side he was a mad man during games and during moments at practice. It was a real Dr. Jekyll and Mr. Hyde type of situation. Many of the players that were already attending Lamar had a difficult time playing for him because of this. The guy that had the hardest time was Eddie Robinson. Eddie was a 6'2, big bodied, strong and athletic PG from Muncie Indiana. Over the years I have heard the stories of the struggle that Eddie had with Mike. He was almost sent home a few times in his first two years at Lamar. I think he was so hard on Eddie for two reasons, he was a point guard and he was smooth. Coaches do not like smooth players. Many of my struggles stemmed from me being smooth. Coaches want their player to "look" like they are playing hard. They want you foaming at the mouth, diving for loose balls you can't get and things like that. I wasn't like that, and neither was Eddie. Mike comes off as a tough hardnosed point guard who was a floor general with some really good leadership skills. I imagine his attitude was Chris Paul like. I am sure he cursed out many of his teammates, because he sure did curse us out.

I have to give a quick history on myself as a player so that you can better understand the experience at Lamar. All my life I heard that I didn't play hard. I didn't know what that meant, but I have a better understanding now. I wasn't blessed with a motor AT ALL. It's kind of frustrating because I wanted to overcome this stigma for my entire career. This issue was a major reason I didn't get any major looks coming out of Santa Rosa. On my stat line alone, 23, 10, 60% from the field, Mid 40's from 3 and 90% from the line, you would think I would have gotten some interest from a low level Pac 12 school. Having been a college coach, there is a certain LOOK that you want to see when you recruit a player. I have super slow feet which made it tough to defend, and I wasn't really athletic as far as foot speed, explosion and vertically. I could dunk of course but I played under the rim. As I reflect, I overcame a lot of physical shortcoming to have a pretty decent career. That just hit me as I wrote all of the issues I battled. I had none of the attributes that coaches look for other than, I was a good kid, and I was highly skilled offensively. Coach Mac was the only coach that I never had to hear these things from, and it's only because I was having the best statistical year in Santa Rosa history.

Mike, being a gritty guy who I am sure had to scrap his ass off to have an impact, hated the way Eddie and I played. We got the business every day in practice and the games were amplified. During games Mike was an entirely different animal. If I were to document all of the stories over those two years this story would never end. I will interject my first Mike Deane story now. We were playing at Southeastern Louisiana one evening. Mike had a lot of pet peeves that would drive him crazy. One of those pet Peeves was giving up a basket right before the half. He thought these were precursors to losing close games. We worked on end of half situations all the time. Most teams if they had a guy they would go 1-4 flat. In a one for flat we would force the ball handler right into a double team and rotate everyone to the strong side leaving the far guy in the corner open. Once a pass was made we were to rotate back. The terminology for it was, force right, rotate, rotate back. We worked on this a lot and never got burned on it. It's a great strategy for a 1-4 flat. This particular game, Terrell forgot to rotate to the corner, so the guy with the ball was able to drive into the double and make an easy pass to the corner in which Terrell was late on his close out and the guy banged the 3 in the corner. Mike was Livid. He runs up to Terrell and begins to yell at him. Mike would always say "we're gonna lose" when one of his pet peeves was broken. As he says this to Terell, T fires back, "No we're not, no we're not, you're always quitting on us, you're always quitting, Let's gooooo!" and sprints to the lock room. I will spare the details of the lock room, nothing really eventful happened, but they had a conversation that lead to Mike saying that if we lost that game, Terrell would be going home. Thankfully we won the game and never had to find out if Mike was serious or not. I will get into a few more stories to paint the picture of the things I dealt with as a player. Lamar was not very good when I got there, but I didn't really feel the pressure to be the savior. In my mind I was a Pac 10 level player in the Southland conference. I was going to lead the country in scoring or die trying. My brother and I have a saying that we both live by, "bust your gun". This means get your shots up at all costs. That's exactly what I did.

My first game was a major disappointment, I thing I had 5 point on 2-7 shooting. We were at Rice in Houston and I don't know if I was nervous or what but I stunk it up. A few nights later we played Texas A&M and this was my coming out party. I had 27 and 11 in a close loss. I took a quick shot late in a one possession game when Mike thought I should have let the game come to me and gotten it later in the clock. He and I had a rational discussion about it. He wasn't mad at me; he wanted me to learn from that moment. When Mike was in his right mind he was a very good teacher of the game. I learned so much and became a much better offensive player under him. The biggest impact he had on my game was the "slide shot". I was a one leg jumper who liked to get all the way to the cup and in turn I would get a lot of charge calls. The slide shot allowed me to get to the cup and avoid charges. I got a number of And 1's over the next two years using the move. In college most teams force you baseline into a charge situation. Once I learned the slide shot I could attack the baseline hard and I got a lot of baskets because of it. Mike was huge on film and game preparation. I learned to prepare on another level at Lamar. He was so detail oriented that it taught me how to watch film, scout opponents, focus on their tendencies, and see how I could attack the opposing team and be effective. This was the days of VHS, so each dorm suite would get their own tape. We would have to watch it at least 3 times before film the next day. Then we would watch the film as a team and he would quiz us on our scouting reports. He would quiz us on opposing players and not just the guys that we were guarding. He really enjoyed teaching the game; I feel like this is why I am such a detailed coach and skill development specialist. I contribute that to Mike Deane. Coach Monson was also very detailed with his scouting reports. That's where I got familiar with learning player tendencies and things of that nature. My being such a student of the game helped me to be successful. Most nights at the D1 level the guy guarding me was quicker, and more athletic, I learned to use that against my defenders. My IQ was the only advantage I had in the physical matchup most nights. The funny thing is that it was natural for me. I can remember being eleven or twelve and thinking about how I would attack my defender next time I caught the ball because of the last possession when he was guarding me. I had great natural instincts, and I could react very quickly. To be a good scorer that's what it takes. You have to process so many elements before catching the ball and then another set of elements after you make the catch. When you think about it it's pretty impressive how much your brain can process and make your body do in a matter of milliseconds. That was my brain and that is why I was able to have the success that I had as a player.

For the next 20 games or so I averages almost 23 points per game and was the leading scorer in the league. Still, every day was a struggle. Mike and I had a rough relationship on the court. He would be screaming at me during the games at it would drive me crazy. He hated that he had to play me because I was scoring the ball so well. He would tell me all the time that "I had him by the balls". He didn't want to have to play me so much because he didn't think I was playing hard enough. It was a struggle and I really wasn't enjoying playing the game anymore. We were hovering around .500 which was much better than we were projected. I believe that they had only won 3 games the previous year and they hadn't won a road game in two years. I remember when we won our first road game at Texas A&M Corpus Christi. Mike and I were having a rough game and even Ron Austin got on me. I can't remember if I was having a hard time guarding or what but they got on me. I ended up hitting a big 3 in the corner, and finishing the game with 20 points. My teammates went crazy in the locker room. Many of them had never won a road game at the D1 level. While they were celebrating I was frustrated in the locker room. I was always very hard on myself. I think that stemmed from my father.

My Dad was a very supportive father. I couldn't have asked for a better parental situation. My dad is the most intelligent man that I know to this day. He retired from the Environmental Protection Agency where he was some type of Chemist. He is 6'5 about 230. To us growing up he was a giant man that commanded a lot of respect. He didn't say much so when he spoke you listened. He came to all of my games and he rarely said much but he would always tell me that I needed to play harder, or I should have had more rebounds. Even when I would drop 25 or so, he would always tell me about the things I could have done better. He would only say a sentence or two, and he wasn't negative about it. He just wanted me to perform better. When I was younger this was hard for me to deal with. I didn't have a complex in which I wanted to please him, nor did I feel like I was letting him down, but I would have liked for him to tell me "good game" more often than he did. Obviously he knows something that I didn't when I was younger and he was only telling me what I needed to hear vs., what I wanted to hear. When I got to Junior College I was able to deal with it better and it was always good to hear his opinion.

Through our relationship I learned to be very hard on myself and set the bar really high. I rarely lived up to my own expectations, and most times my coaches would think that I was mad at them when they would come down on me. I would be more mad at myself then they ever could be. As I sat in the locker room while my teammates celebrated I beat myself up, and wouldn't allow myself to be happy. I had come from championship programs so winning on the road was something I never had trouble doing. I could not relate to that feeling. In the midst of this scoring tear that I was on I caught food poisoning while we were in Arlington. I still don't know what I ate but it ripped my stomach to shreds. I was literally running off of the court to throw up in a garbage can during free throws and such. It was rough, I couldn't hold any food and I had a five point game. Anyone that understands how scoring averages work in a twenty-six game season, a five point game is a killer. We played Thursday and Saturday in our league. The next game I was still feeling the effects of the food poisoning. My body had very little energy and I had 11 points that game. That weekend dropped my scoring average quite a few points. For the rest of the season I was up and down. I never really got my rhythm back and during that stretch my guy Ron Austin emerged as another key scorer. Ron was a 6'2 shooting guard with crazy bounce out of Brother Rice High School in Detroit. The same high school Hayes had come from. Ron was the link to Hayes coming to Lamar. Their families were close and Ron was influential in Hayes coming down. As I played very inconsistent ball down the stretch Ron was playing very well, he even made 2 game winning buckets. I can remember the papers asking me about my performance and I told them flat out that I needed to play better. I felt like the games we lost were on me as the leader of the team. I wore it all on my chest. I understood why they brought me into the program and I was fully aware that I would get the blame if I didn't play well and we lost. Again, I was never the same after being sick, I don't know if getting sick took that much of a toll on my body but I wasn't the same guy.

I ended up averaging just under 18 per night and third in the league in scoring. I was on track for newcomer of the year as well as a first team All-Conference. I doubt that I would have been the league MVP because we finished 4th in the league. We were projected in the pre season to finish last so we did surprise some teams. We lost to McNeese State in the Semi finals of the conference tournament. In the post game Mike challenged me in front of the team in his sarcastic and mind jarring manner. He essentially told me that my individual accolades would mean nothing if we didn't win. He said I'd be in the running for preseason league MVP, and I'd be a thousand point scorer but It wouldn't mean anything if we didn't win. I felt where he was coming from and I couldn't be mad. That's what I had signed up for. I want to end this with another Mike Deane story for some amusement. Mike had rules about our appearance, and how we kept ourselves. This was the era of the cornrows and headbands and things of that nature. I had to cut my hair before I went down there which to me was no big deal. A lot of the fellas wanted to grow their hair out because they had not been able to for the 2 previous years because of Mike's rules about hair. I had cornrows on my visit, so Eddie and Ron grew their hair out and had braids in hopes that Mike would let them keep them because he recruited me when I had mine. They were so disappointed when I showed up and my hair was gone. Fast forward to the season. We also could not have facial hair other that a mustache. As young men, especially young men of color, our forms of self expression come out through our hair and facial hair. Hayes was a bit of a pretty boy and a bit rebellious. I am not sure if Mike was being lenient or Hayes was just feeling ballsy, but he showed up with the chinstrap beard on game day. I have to preface this story by saying Hayes averaged less than 5 minutes per game up to this point and had very little bearing on whether we won or lost that year. Not according to Mike on this day. We take a tough home loss and we are all sitting in the locker room waiting on Mike and the coaches to come in and give the post game speech. I can't remember all of the details of why we lost that game but I am sure it had nothing to do with Hayes, and then suddenly it had everything to do with Hayes. Mike starts ranting saying "Hayes this is all your fault, you and that (expletive) beard. You don't want to buy in. None of you guys want to buy in". When coaches say things sometimes in post game rants, as a team we think that coaches are crazy and we at times have to hold in our laughter. We were thinking, "he can't be blaming this game on Hayes right now". At this point in my life I understand what he was saying, but the way he framed it was hilarious. He blamed us losing on Hayes' Beard. Classic Mike Deane.

Chapter 6: Summer Summer Summer Time.

That summer I stayed in Texas and took some classes. I also had the opportunity to work with one of the boosters, Bobby James, who owned a medical clothing and supply store. Mike was against it, but I needed some money to feed myself. Mike knew that it would take away from my time in the gym and he knew how important it was to my growth that I come back a much better player. There was a huge turning point with the school and the program during this time. Legendary Coach Billy Tubbs was hired as the Athletic Director. Coach Tubbs is a hall of fame college coach that had started his coaching career at Lamar. Essentially, he was coming home to help the program turn the corner. This obviously caused a conflict within the program because I don't know how much Mike cared for Coach Tubbs, but also I am sure Mike began to feel some pressure. I will come back to this situation later. Eddie was really close with Bobby James and he also worked that summer at the same place I was working. We worked around our summer school schedule if I can remember correctly, I am pretty sure we went in everyday after our classes got out. Our job was to deliver medical supplies to patients in the work van. It was an easy job except for the fact that there were no GPS services for us and we had to use yahoo maps to get our routes together. We would get lost sometimes and have to call for directions but that was the biggest issue we had with the job. We used to deliver oxygen tanks, depends, shower chairs and things of that nature. We didn't get off until 6 pm every day which wasn't pleasing to Mike either. I am pretty sure this was the last thing he wanted to see, Eddie and Me working until 6pm the summer before our senior year. Eddie and I became real close that summer. We would work out after we got off of work but the coaches would be gone so we didn't get to put in a lot of work with them. I did spend a lot of time in the weight room that summer and I got a lot stronger. I recall Ron having us do this crazy bench press workout that he had gotten from his trainer in Detroit. As much as we tried to improve, Mike was absolutely right about us not being able to handle that load with school and work so that summer we did not improve as much as we could and should have.

I also had the pleasure to go to Australia with a traveling team that summer. This was my first time out of the country. Eddie and I went with a collection of players from around the U.S. It was a good group of guys and we only lost one game while we were out there. We played against a ton of pro teams from over there and the majority of them were very unimpressive. We were a bunch of low and mid-major players, few of which were all conference and we were in control of most of the games, until we ran into the National team. They put a beating on us like no other. Shane Heal, legendary player in Australia who got into it with Charles Barkley during the 1992 Olympics, played for this team. He was older but still pretty much their lead guy. He gave us the works that day. So much in fact that he showered and put on his street clothes at half time and sat out the rest of the game. That was the most helpless that I had ever felt as a basketball player. They were bigger, faster, more skilled and more seasoned than us. It was a great experience to get to play against those guys. Even though they beat the brakes off of us.

The best player we played against out there wasn't even on the national team. He played for a regular pro team there because they said he was a bit unstable. But this dude could GO! I have no idea what is name is, all I remember was him getting bucket after bucket after bucket. He was about 6'6, 230 maybe 240 all muscle. He had a motor out of the world and could jump out of the gym. He had about 7 bang outs (I didn't us dunk because that wouldn't serve these plays any justice). He was cramming the ball through the hoop with all the strength in his body. This dude was a machine. He was taking guys off the bounce, posting and scoring on the block, making jump shots, spinning baseline and dunking on our bigs. He had the total package and was by far the best player we faced while we were there. We asked why he wasn't playing for their top team and many of the locals said that he was a bit crazy. He was a player that seemed to like conflict, and he did play like he was crazy. He was grunting, and making all kind of noises during the game. He was scowling at guys and pushing some guys on our team. I could definitely see that there was a screw loose with this one, but I respect him as a basketball player for sure. He left us no choice.

All in all it was a great experience. I got a chance to see what is may be like to play overseas after I graduated. I competed pretty well. Our team was very balanced so the scoring was spread pretty even. My biggest thing when I went over there was to play hard. I really did concentrate on that and for the most part I was successful. I played harder than I ever had and Mike noticed. He consistently told me that he noticed a difference in my effort and that I was moving quicker than I ever had. That was reassuring to hear from him because I knew that was his biggest issue with me. I knew that if I could increase my motor that he would lay off of me a little bit. I was tired of him screaming at me all game long. We won all of our games except the one game against the national team and I got to meet and play with some cool dudes. I don't recall if I got to go home that summer or not but if I did it wasn't for long. Pretty soon it was back to business as usual, and my senior year was about to begin.

Chapter 7: Pressure Busts Pipes

"Pressure is a word that is misused in our vocabulary.
When you start thinking of pressure, its because you
started to think of failure."
Tommy Lasorda

Going into my senior year, expectations were high for the Lamar Cardinals. We had a new AD, we were senior heavy, and we had a solid recruiting class. I had set some high expectations for myself and the team as well. I wanted to lead the country in scoring and be Conference Player of the Year. I also wanted for us to win the conference and make the NCAA tournament. I felt like these were all reasonable expectations and well within my capabilities, and the capabilities of our team. We were returning our entire starting five. We had a solid recruiting class with some very talented Freshman. The first curve ball happened on media day. Mike got in front of the media and started talking about how he was going to run the offense through Brian Rowan. Brian was a 7 footer who played sparing minutes the previous year. He was entering his junior year and showed very little signs that he could be a lead guy. He never once had a good practice the year before and from what the fellas and I could surmise from the open gyms that we had, it didn't seem like much had changed. We were dumbfounded, and the seniors like Eddie, Ron and I were insulted. We didn't say anything about it, and we knew that this wouldn't last long since one of the freshman, Jason Grant, a 6'9 kid from Canada with some good back to the basket moves and some exceptional shot blocking capabilities, was kicking his butt in open gyms every day. We paid no mind until practice started and he had changed the offense and was really trying to feature Brian. Brian was a nice guy, but when you're 7 feet and playing low D1 ball it's obvious that you have a lot of short comings as a basketball player. He couldn't average double figures in a gym by himself. Mike was really trying to feature him and I believe that this threw off the chemistry of the team. Eddie, Ron and Terrell had spent 4 years in the program and they were the remaining players from Mike's original recruiting class. This was a slap in the face to them and to me as well. Although I had only been there a year, I felt like I had put in enough work the previous year to have the offense featured around myself and the other seniors. That is what he came into my living room and told me, and that was the reason I chose Lamar over all the other schools. As we continued to practice, the fellas and I got increasingly more frustrated with Mike making us feed the ball to a guy who was not a scorer. This did not make for a good preseason for us. With all the expectations that were placed on us, and that I had placed upon myself, this threw everything out of whack. I wasn't playing well, and the team wasn't performing up to our expectations.

Along with everything that was going on with the offense, Mike was a bit more harsh than he had been the previous year. I think he felt the heat coming from above with Coach Tubbs being the new AD. I think Mike felt like we had to perform well or he would lose his job. Having spent some time coaching at the D1 level, I understand the pressures of job security, or lack thereof in the business. This is one of the most cut throat fields to work in. It's a "what have you done for me lately" type of deal for most coaches. I was told that 99% of the guys in this business are "hired to be fired". For the most part this is a very true statement. There are very few guys in this business that have job security and Mike was not one of them. He knew it and so did we. He was increasingly more intolerable with us, and was even stronger with his language that year. I wasn't playing well at all and the more I struggled, the more pressure I started to put on myself and the worse I played. It was a vicious cycle. Mike called me into his office one day and asked me if I had personal issues going on, and I had nothing for him. I just couldn't put it together. I wanted to be so good that I was awful. I was letting my guys down, once again, and I was letting myself down. I was letting my friends, family and Vallejo down.

That year we played at the University of Pacific in Stockton, CA early in the season. It may have even been the first game of the year. This was the game Mike scheduled for my family to come and see me. The family came out, and I stunk it up. One of my worst games I have ever played. I don't know if it was the pressure of being at home, or all the other factors, but it was pretty bad. We lost a close game, and had I played well we probably win that game. After the game the coach from UOP congratulates me and says he should have recruited me. Hind sight is 20/20 I always say. I felt the pressure mounting that year and it ate away at me daily.

I remember one day at practice stretching in our circle, Mike mentioned to me that boosters were asking him "how much would it cost for a one-way ticket to California?" I broke down in the middle of practice. At this point I was very fragile when it came to my performance. I was always an emotional person, as a child I cried a lot when I didn't succeed. Everyone would tell me that I was too emotional and when I got old enough to control it I shut my emotions down. I became emotionless and my coaches began to hate that. I guess I came off as apathetic. I was just doing what my coaches and everyone else had told me to do. That day was the tipping point. I had held in so much for so long that it came out in that moment. It wasn't a breakdown physically, I shed a tear or two and that was it but inside I was broken. My play was inconsistent, my minutes diminished, and we were underperforming, mainly because I was.

This year was a bit of a soap opera for the program. It started with one of our fellow seniors deciding to Red-shirt because of personal reasons. Terrell Pettaway was a big part of our team the year before and would have eventually become a starter once the Brian Rowan experiment was over. He was a 6'7 forward with long arms and a great motor. He was a good shot blocker, and the previous year had dunked on the top 2 shot blockers in the country, Wojciech Myrda, who is still second all time in career blocks, and D'or Fischer who actually led the NCAA that year. He would have been a big part of our team and we really missed him. We also had a really good freshman guard Jonathon "JB" Burnet, god rest his soul, tare his ACL. He was a really good scoring guard off the bench. Another scoring guard named Tyler Hackstadt, 6'2 athletic guard who could also shoot it, got hurt that year as well. The icing on the cake that year was Brian Rowan actually quit the team mid way through the season for personal reasons. Isn't that the most ironic thing you have ever heard? Mike was trying to build the team around a guy who didn't even want to play. The only person that flourished that season was Ron. Ron and I were left to do the bulk of the scoring. He balled out that year. Through all the adversity and commotion that was going on around the team he was doing his thing. Ron and I both ended up averaging just under 16 points per game but he was much more efficient than I was that year. I struggled. Needless to say we didn't accomplish any of our team goals and I was way off of my individual goals. I had succumbed to the pressures that were surrounding me. My senior year was a failure, and it was all because I couldn't handle it. My two years at Lamar, I didn't come close to what I had expected of myself, although I was All-conference both years, I was still very disappointed in myself.

Once the season was over Mike was fired and the staff was forced to look for another job. Coach Tubbs was named head coach just like everyone figured would happen. In the midst of all of this I was being contacted by some agents about playing overseas. It was something I had always wanted to do but after hearing the horror stories from my brother about not getting all of his money and things of that nature, I didn't know if I wanted to pursue it. I really didn't have any other plans beyond college. Playing ball was all I had wanted to do and I figured I would play for as long as I could and worry about life after basketball later. Later came sooner than I had anticipated.

Chapter 8: Welcome to the real world kid!
"The real world doesn't always greet with a warm welcome"
Uknown

A few days after receiving my degree in General studies from Lamar, I moved home. I decided not to pursue playing ball over seas. I was burned out by my playing experience and I didn't really feel like I wanted to play competitively anymore. Upon my return to Vallejo, I decided I wanted to get into coaching. I had to figure out what I wanted to do with my career. In the meantime my mother suggested I take the CBEST so I could start substitute teaching while I looked for work. At the same time I knew I wanted to get into coaching so I went down to my Alma Mater (Vallejo High) and asked if I could help out with the team. Duke Brown was the coach at the time. Duke was a long time local coach, and had succeeded my coach, Vic Wallace. Duke was a former college football player at Fresno State. He had some early success inheriting a team with some good athletes and an All-American in Demarcus Nelson. Demarcus Nelson was 6'3 athletic, and very strong combo guard who committed to Duke after his sophomore season. He ended up becoming California's all time leading scorer and also in the top 5 in rebounds. A very talented kid who I had known since he was a young boy, having played little league with his older brother Darnell. Demarcus left Vallejo and transferred to Sheldon High school in Sacramento before heading to play for Coach K. This current Vallejo team still had some talent and a good leadership. The best player on the team, Amos Carter, was a 6'3 freak athlete with some skills. He was arguably one of the best pure athletes to ever come through Vallejo. He was an all-league player that went to college for basketball, changed sport and was an All-state wide receiver, who caught 4 touchdowns against San Francisco City who was one of the top teams in the nation. Amos led this team to Arco Arena where we lost to current NBA player Ryan Anderson and Oak Ridge High. My first year as a coach was a great experience. Coach Duke allowed me to do a lot with the guys and I was able to grow as a coach. I still hadn't really found my identity as a coach yet and though Coach Duke was a good guy I really didn't learn much under him. It wasn't because he wasn't a good coach but he didn't play basketball after high school. I had the opportunity to play for and learn from four different college coaches, so I was at a higher level of thinking. I had seen every type of practice imaginable, as well as game prep and game plan that you could imagine other that the NBA level. But it was a good experience.

When it came to my professional life, this was the beginning of the floundering. I had visions of becoming a fire fighter when I got out of school. I was told that the first step was to enroll in an EMT class and get my certification. I attended a night class at Solano College in Fairfield, which was about 10 minutes from my house in Vallejo. The class was pretty easy, but there were some times that conflicted with basketball. I missed a few games but I also chose to miss a few classes. As I continue with the story there will be many instances in which I picked basketball over some things that were probably more important at the time. This was the first of many. I missed on class and ended up missing a passing grade by a small margin. The teacher emailed me and was going to allow me to attend one class the following semester and I would be good to go. I have absolutely no recollection of why I didn't take her up on this offer but in the end I did not receive my EMT certification. This was the beginning of many attempts at employment in my search for life after basketball.

The next few years were much of the same. I was still subbing and coaching at Vallejo High School with Coach Duke. In the meantime, my girlfriend from College moved from Texas to Vallejo and we got our own place. This didn't last very long. We were too young and once we moved in with one another things began to break down. I wasn't ready to be in a serious relationship and we were much different in our personalities. I was 24 at the time and it was way too early to be trying to settle down, especially since I hadn't established myself career wise. Obviously we broke up but we remained cordial with one another. She went on to move out and started teaching in Vallejo, and then Fairfield. I was still trying to figure things out.

In October of 2004, I crossed into the land of Omega Psi Phi. I was initiated into the Fraternity October 30th, and it was one of the greatest moments of my life. I was raised in a household in which my parents were both part of Greek Letter Organizations. Fraternities, and sororities are defined as: A group of people sharing a common profession or interest. It can be better explained as a brotherhood that shares the same ideal and vision. Part of being in a frat is of course fraternizing. Once a month we would meet up at the local Applebee's for our "First Fridays" event. These evenings consisted of good conversations and food and drinks. The night was coming to an end and there were just three of us left just hanging out. This is when I laid my eyes on the love of my life for the very first time. The fellas and I were talking, maybe watching some basketball on TV and she walked in. I immediately noticed her, and thinking out loud to the fellas I said, "Who is that?" My fraternity Brother Edison Kelly turns and says "That's my cousin". I immediately perk up and say, "Let's go meet your cousin." The three of us stroll over to their table. She was grabbing something to eat with her cousin. I introduce myself and use Ed as a buffer.

Could this situation have been more perfect? I was taken back by her beauty. Her gorgeous hair, beautiful skin, and captivating eyes that glistened like a crystal chandelier. I was my usual charming self while Chanee remained engaged yet standoffish. The conversation turned to cuisine. Her love of food and the different types of cuisine seemed to be an agreeable topic. So I went with it, and we had an extensive conversation about ethnic food. They'd decided upon Ethiopian. I had never had Ethiopian but I wouldn't let her know this, and I knew Berkeley had several Ethiopian places, so that's where I kept the conversation. This proved to be beneficial. The night ended, and we parted ways without exchanging information. All I had was her name. The following day I got on the computer and went on MySpace. I hadn't gotten the correct spelling of her name but I was able to find her profile, and I wrote two words to her. "Ethiopian anyone?" We had an instant connection, and dated for a few months but ended up going our separate ways, or so we thought.

In 2006, Duke stepped down for personal reasons and I became the interim head coach at Vallejo. This was a dream come true for me that quickly turned into a nightmare. I wasn't ready to run a program. From a basketball standpoint I was, but I hadn't really taken into consideration the off the court issues I would face. Coaching at public school at this time was very different. Coach Wallace would often tell me that the reason he stepped down was because the kids were not serious about basketball and that it had become too stressful. Coaching wasn't worth the headache for him so he walked away from it. He started doing skill development and was doing very well financially on the side with his business. That was my first introduction to personal skill development. Nonetheless, I thought I was up for the challenge.

That year was filled with ups and downs. Neither point guard made grades, one of my players was a head case and kept getting in trouble and my best player was coming off of knee surgery and wasn't fully healthy. Needless to say we struggled through the first part of the year going 2-8. Amidst all of this I had finally gotten a full time teaching position at this charter school in Vallejo, Mare Island Technology Academy. It was a really cool place to work. The staff was very passionate about providing alternative, project based education to the young people. It was a middle and high school. Originally I was hired in a math support position. On the day I showed up to sign my papers, they put me into a full time teaching position at the middle school. They had just lost their Pre-Algebra teacher and needed someone to come on board. I was excited about the opportunity, and more about the financial stability and the benefits. Even with all of the struggles I was in a good place for the first time in a long time. In order for me to take the job I had to enroll in a credential program. My mother had been asking me to do so but I had no interest in becoming a teacher so there was no need for me to do so in my mind. I enrolled at Tuoro University in Vallejo. The program was new so there were some kinks that needed to be worked out. I ended up finishing my course work but I washed out of the program mainly because I didn't want to be a teacher. I stayed at MIT for two years, teaching math. I moved up to the high school after the first semester in which I started working there. There was a teacher who went out on maternity leave and I took over her Geometry and Algebra II classes. This experience was very difficult. I learned that I didn't really like teaching and that I needed to get out of the classroom. In the midst of all of this, we ended up closing out the year on a strong note and finishing one game behind Rodriguez for the league title. We lost to Hogan, our cross town rival on an awful call down the stretch. I hate referees, I think most of them at the high school level are horrible, and do more messing up the game then they do maintain the order and integrity of the game. We were down one point with under 10 seconds left. I drew up a fade play against the 2-3 zone with some slip action. We execute to perfection, and get Aaron Mcgee, our leading scorer the ball in the short corner to attack the basket. Those who know me, know that I teach every one of my players the slide shot now. It's a great move. Aaron had worked on his slide shot tirelessly and attacked the baseline, planted his foot, slid past the defender, made a little contact but so little that the defender didn't even fall down. The ref blows his whistle, and what do you know. He puts his hand behind his head and calls a damn offensive foul. I lost it. Aaron made the shot and should have been shooting free throws. Instead he picks up an offensive foul and we lose the game, don't get a share of the league title, and don't make the playoffs because of our poor start. So if you watch me coach now, you understand my disdain for referees. There is another incident later in this story that will make it even more clear as to why I hate referees, except the homie Renee Robinson, she's solid.

In 2005 I was asked by a spiritual mentor of mine to coach an AAU team. At this time I was against AAU. I felt it fostered bad habits, it wasn't real basketball, and that is was overall a very detrimental part of these kids' development. I was on the fence about it for a while but finally he convinced me. After working with me for a few weeks, he was also the one who insisted I get into Skill development. Carl thought that I was a very good teacher of the game and that I should get into the business. He thought that I could be special. I did a couple of workouts with him but I didn't really take it seriously. I agreed to coach with the Oakland Soldiers, an organization started in the Bay Area by Calvin Andrews (current NBA agent) and Hashim Ali Alauddeen (Current professor at Cal Berkeley). This was a well respected AAU program that had put out some of the Bay Area's best talent. Players like Eddie House, Leon Powe, Ryan Anderson and such. Even Lebron James and Brandon Jennings had played in several tournaments with the Soldiers. It was growing in popularity and because of the camouflage uniforms the program stood out at the national tournaments. All of the top kids in the bay wanted to play for the soldiers. Carl convinced me to take this team using the fact that I would have gotten a chance to coach my God Brother Desmond Simmons. I had known Desmond since he was born and had watched him grow into a pretty good basketball player. He had wanted to work with me for years

My first team was organized by Carl. He recruited the players and was handling the parents. He scheduled the practices and intercepted any issues that could possibly come my way. If you know anything about coaching AAU, then you know that there are a multitude of issues that arise during the course of the spring and summer. This year went off without a hitch. We over achieved, all of the players and parents were happy for the most part. This created a false sense of reality for me. I thought because this year had gone so smoothly that this was the norm for an AAU season. Not so much. I would never have thought that this would lead to another series of painful events that fuel my love and hate for the game all at the same time.

Chapter 9: **The pursuit of Happiness.**

I love coaching the game of basketball. It brings me almost as much joy as playing. There is nothing like playing the game of basketball to me. I don't want to say that there is nothing that can bring me as much joy because there have been moments in life that I have experienced equal amounts of joy. I learned that being in love can take you to me to the heights that basketball could in certain moments. I had been searching for those moments for a long time at this point. I fell in love with coaching, and teaching the game of basketball. I fell in love with training and working with kids. I began to pursue a career in college coaching in 2008. That was the year I figured out what I wanted to do with my life. I hadn't been passionate about many things in life up to this point, especially since I had stopped playing. I had worked a bunch of jobs, entered a few academic programs that I didn't finish, and hadn't really put down any roots. This was it. I wanted to be a legendary college basketball coach.

My journey began in the middle of an AAU season when I got a call from my old Coach Mike Deane. Mike was the head coach at Wagner College in New York. They had a third assistant coaching position open and I was being highly considered for the position. I flew out to New York to interview with Mike and his staff. When I flew out there I stayed with the Assistant Coach Kenyon Spears. Kenyon was a Lamar Graduate and was on the staff my two years at Lamar. He and I had a really good relationship and I believe he was the one who put me on to the vacant position. This was also my first time going to New York so I could kill two birds with one stone. The evening I touched down, Kenyon came to get me from the airport and we drove back to his spot. I had a big day scheduled the following day so I got this spot and crashed. After a good night's sleep, I had my interview that morning. It was less of an interview and more of a detailed job description of what the job would be. I had such a good relationship with Mike and K that it was more of a conversation. I was green to college coaching so they were laying out what my duties would be. They knew my background, my character, and more importantly, they knew me. I came to learn that this business is ALL about relationships. That's the only reason I was able to get the interview. Coaches like to hire former players, and for many it's their introduction into the business. The interview was very informal. Mike was an informal person for the most part. He actually made all of the people the interviewed wear Polos. Had it not been Mike, and had I not had a previous relationship I still would have worn a suit. Because I knew him and how he operated I wore a polo. After the interview he scheduled an open gym in which I got a chance to play with the guys. This was a good way for me to get familiar with the kids and to show them that I could still do my thing. I was killing in that open gym. I was the best player in the gym. Still at the age of 28 years old, the fact that I could still dominate a college open gym was very satisfying to me. I played so well Mike asked me why I wasn't playing overseas. I laughed it off, I didn't want to tell him that he was the last piece of the puzzle that sucked the last bit of enjoyment that I got out of playing the game right out of me. After the open gym I was able to spend some time with the players. They seemed excited that I could possibly be joining the staff. They were impressed by my play in the open gym and told me that they would love to have me on the staff. This gave me a nice boost in my confidence, I doubt that Mike would bring someone else in that could still outplay the majority of the kids on the team. I had a great experience that day and felt good walking away from the process.

The rest of the weekend I pretty much spent exploring New York. I had a few friends that lived out there at the time so we were able to connect. I linked up with my friend Kourtney from College. She and I hadn't seen each other since we attended Lamar together. I got us some tickets to the Yankee game and we were able to catch a game. It was scorching that day. I remember Kourtney had an umbrella and thank God she did because We would have cooked if she hadn't. After the game we linked up with some other friends of mine and went to dinner. After dinner we hit the town. We went to a rooftop lounge, and then to a late night diner and then I took the ferry back to Kenyon's house and shut it down for the night.

I returned home after the weekend feeling like I had done well enough to get the job. My relationship with Mike and Kenyon certainly gave me a leg up on the competition. I was expecting to hear from mike after a couple of days. After not hearing from Mike for a few days I got worried and text Kenyon to ask him what the deal was. He said Mike had been trying to contacting me for the last couple of days. I had two phones at the time and for some reason they had been trying to contact me on my alternative phone which was never turned on. I powered it on; Mike had left several messages for me to call him. As soon as I heard his message I called him and this was my introductory conversation to the politics involved with college coaching. During the interview process Mike was open and honest about what was going on at the school, and that his job was hinging on whether he won or not the upcoming season. He told me that they had some talent but that they were young. Young teams do not win and the low/mid major level. You need older guys and experience to win at that level. You will rarely have a freshman or sophomore that is an impact player. He could see the writing on the wall and he knew that the AD would have some say so in the end. As we began our conversation he cut to the chase. That is one thing that I will always love and respect about Mike. He was a straight shooter. He rarely bit his tongue or pulled any punches. He told you plain and simple, as any man should. He told me that he went to the AD and told him that I was his choice. The Athletic Director had a different idea. He made him hire an Alumnus of the program who was a respected player in the program just a few years prior. Getting hired at you Alma Mater is also a great way to get into the business, and sometimes will trump having a relationship with the head coach. In this instance, since Mike and the staff were on the hot seat, the AD flexed his muscle, and I was out of a job opportunity. This was the first of many times where I learned the college coaching game was a cold one. I was given a false sense of security in this instance because I was able to get an interview so easily. I figured it would work like this whenever a job came available in which I knew the coach. I figured with all the turnover that happens every March, I would be able to get a job in no time. Little did I know that this business is a buddy buddy business that went far beyond my level of comprehension at the time. It is highly competitive, a good old boy network, and in some cases you have to sell your soul to get in.

At this point I am in full pursuit of a college job. I was beginning to understand the politics of the business and was willing to participate to a certain extent. I understood that working with the Soldiers would help me build my network of coaches that may help me get a job down the road. In 2009 I was coaching a really good team that had some high level recruits like Nick Johnson and Jabari Brown, both of which are currently in the NBA. This was my first time really having kids that I could see were going to be NBA level players. This was also the first time we would play against kids that would be NBA level players as well. Most of my kids were in their Sophomore year so we were a year younger than most teams on the circuit. We performed really well that year. That was a great AAU season for the Oakland Soldiers. Even though they were nationally known, none of the teams had really made as much noise as we had. Nike was trying to monopolize all of the top players on the circuit and they were changing their format. That summer was a precursor to the current Elite Youth Basketball League (EYBL). We played against kids that would go on to Duke, North Carolina, Texas and many more top schools. This was an amazing experience; I got to see AAU basketball on an entirely different level. This was the moment I changed my view on AAU basketball. Seeing the top players face one another made me see the value in elite level AAU. I still struggle with AAU at the local level, and think kids play too many games, but that's a different conversation. This was worth it for the players and we weren't playing a ton of games, so the kids were able to get their skill work in during the AAU breaks. The director of the Soldiers was and still is Mark Olivier. Mark had been running the program for nearly 20 years and was the main catalyst in building the program to where it was. He made it a nationally recognized program along with some help behind the scenes. He was a master recruiter and became a mentor of mine. I relied on him heavily to understand the business that was AAU, as well as the college coaching landscape. Although we have a very different lens on the game of basketball, he gave me the game on how I could get into college coaching. I was stubborn and didn't fully take his advice, but I did hear what he was saying to me. He assembled some of the most legendary Soldier team, including a team that had Lebron James, Kendrick Perkins, and Leon Powe, three of the top 10 players in the class of 2003. Mark was instrumental in growing the program to where it had been at this point, recruiting other NBA player from out of the area like Brandon Jennings to play with the Soldiers for certain tournaments. Mark was a major player and had some leverage with college coaches because he had all of the players on the West Coast. I could have used the Mark card to get a job I am sure but I was strong in my stance against using any kid from the program or my relationship with Mark to get a job. I figured my basketball acumen, the relationships I built and my ability to show what I could do on the circuit in front of the coaches would be enough to land a job. I was very wrong

Around this time I heard that the National Collegiate Athletic Association (NCAA) put in a rule concerning AAU coaches and employment at the college level. It was also around this time that Chanee came back into my life and we began to rekindle our love for one another. The summer of 2010 was the year that the Oakland soldiers became a premier program in the country. Our roster was not only loaded with almost all high major prospects, we were exciting to watch. We had 4 of the most electric guards in the country.

Our roster consisted of, Josiah Turner, a 6'3 point guard with silky smooth handle, a hesitation out of the world, vision like Jason Kidd and the ability to get anywhere on the floor that he wanted to. Josiah at the time was ranked the number two point guard in the entire country. In my eyes he was the most special of all of the players because he had this natural instinct, and everything came so easily to him. He never got sped up, and he was always in control of his body and the game. He would make the most difficult plays look effortless, that is why I say he was the most special of this super talented bunch.

We also had Nick Johnson, a 6'3 combo guard out of Arizona who could jump out of the gym. Nick was on the team the previous year as well. He transferred from his local high school AZ to Findlay Prep in Vegas. Coach Mike Peck must have put some magic potion in his water because he came back an entirely different kid. He was one of the best defensive guards on the circuit that summer. He was always a really good offensive player, but the fact that his defense had caught up to his offense made us very dangerous because I could have him guard bigger players when we went to a four guard lineup. Nick had a really great summer for us; he did a lot a bit of everything every single game. Nick had grown so much as a player after his year at Findlay, that it made me a believer in what they were doing over there. Aside from all that, there were few guards who could finish on the break like he could. He's a "look out below" guy, a guy that you don't want to jump with.

The next guard we had was Jabari Brown, a 6'4 scoring machine. Jabari was one of the top scorers in the EYBL that summer. He was putting up crazy numbers every single game. I had been coaching Jabari since the summer of his 8th grade year. I knew the first time I put the ball in his hands on a 1-4 flat play at the end of the game that he was going to be a problem. Jabari is a silky smooth pure scorer, who always played with a chip on his shoulder. He never smiled on the court and always looked mad. He hated that California had the "soft" stigma and he tried to disprove it every night out. That's why he never smiled. He and I had a really good relationship because of our history together, and I saw a lot of myself in him. He could score from anywhere on the court but at times it looked like he was cruising. A lot of coaches would tell me that it looked like he wasn't playing hard, but I would explain that he was just smooth. As I explained earlier, coaches do not like smooth. But nonetheless they still recruited him because he was one of the best pure scorers in the country. I would tell Jabari all the information that the coaches would give me because I had been there, and heard all of the same criticisms. I spent extra time on him because I felt like I could give him enough advice about how to break down those barriers that may come his way like they had come in my direction. I would tell him that he was a much better player when attacking the rim, because he had a tendency to be a floater and settle for jump shots. I would tell him to rebound more because a lot of times we were playing with 4 guards and he was the second biggest guy out there, and when you rebound it make you a lot more active and coaches can't say you're not working. I would tell him to get eight free throw attempts per game because that meant he was attacking the rim. He had the best summer of anyone offensively and got MVP of the inaugural Fab 48 tournament in Las Vegas in which we were the champions.

Our next impact player was a 6'9 kid from Oregon named

Kyle Wiltjer. Kyle had been with the program for 3 years now and had grown into a hell of a player. He was a perfect fit for our team because he was a big that could shoot the lights out. With the guards that we had it was important for us to be able to space the floor out and have driving gaps. Kyle allowed us to do that and pull bigs away from the basket. Kyle was also very good with his back to the basket so we dumped it down to him a lot that summer. Kyle was deadly from behind the arc, and most of the bigs on the circuit were really athletic but could not navigate the perimeter like he could. He played on the perimeter at his high school the majority of the time so that was his domain. Kyle gave us some balance and ended up being our only McDonalds All-American off of that team, and one of only 2 players west of the Mississippi. That's when I learned about that voting process and how biased and tainted it was. Kyle deserved it having won 4 state titles in Oregon, but I could have made an argument for Jabari, Nick and Josiah as well. Nonetheless we were happy to get the one we did get. Kyle probably had a better summer the previous one, but the overall team success allowed for him to get a scholarship to play for Coach Calipari at Kentucky and get a national championship, so I am sure he wasn't to upset.

We also had Brandon Ashley, a 6'8 forward that did a little bit of everything. Brandon was a good finisher on and break and around the rim. He ran the floor well and with the guards we had that was pretty much all he needed to do. He had some moves with his back to the basket, and could make an open mid range jumper. I remember his best game being a game against the Belmont Shores who at the time had Grant Garrett, another Arizona Commit. He went at Grant and outplayed him that night. He played harder than I had ever seen him play and he went to work. Brandon had a very good summer with us that year even though he was a year younger than the players mentioned above. He would go on to be a McDonald's All-American the following year.

We also had some really good ancillary players such as

Richard Longrus, a 6'7 "do it all" kind of player. A perfect complement to our team as the third big, and he was a great defender with a high IQ and a good skill set (Washington State). Chuks Iroegbu was a 6'4 strong and athletic guard out of Sacramento. He was also a good defender and could finish with the best of them. Then there was Dominic Artis, an electric guard who would end up one of the top guards in the country the following year. He was a lights out shooter with a handle like very few. It was hard for me to find minutes for Dom because the 4 guards in front of him were 4 of the best in the country. Dom went on to destroy the circuit the following year and lead that Soldiers to being one of the best teams in the country.

Finally, I had to save this young fella for last because he was the talk of the circuit that year. A 5'7 kid out of Oakland California named Keyondre "Kiwi" Gardner was the most exciting player on the circuit that year. Kiwi was a hardnosed kid with a heart the size of Oakland California. We were must see TV, but when this kid was on the court you could not take your eyes off of him. At 5'7 the kid bang out, finish in the paint, get anywhere on the floor that he wanted to, and guard it for 94 feet. He is every coach's dream at the PG. He was constantly talking, he was a great teammate, he kept the game exciting, and most of all he was very passionate about winning. He would constantly do things that made the crowd roar, or OOOH and AAAAH! I would take this kid anywhere in the world with me and match him up against the best of the best. My favorite memory of Kiwi was when we player Indy Speice.
Speice had the top point guard in the country that year in Marquise Teague, and he was KILLING the EYBL. He was one of the top scorers and was making highlights out of anyone who tried to guard him. He was banging out on bigs and dropping mid 30's almost every game. Kiwi was adamant about guarding him. Nick and Jabari wanted to start the game on him, but Kiwi won that argument. Kiwi was the heart and soul of that team. He was the pulse. His energy and toughness permeated throughout the rest of the guys. I am not slighting Nick, Jabari, and Josiah, they were

obviously the guys that were the most talented of the group, but Kiwi was the DOG, and the alpha male of the group. So the ball goes up for the opening tip, I can't remember who won the tip but I think they did. Teague gets the ball, and Kiwi is "IN HIS SHIT"! He rips Teague and goes down for a lay-up. Spiece takes it out and Kiwi picks him up full court again, and right around half court, he rips him again for and takes it for a lay-up. The next trip down, Kiwi is pressuring Teague and he dribbles it off his foot and it goes out of bounds, Soldiers ball. They call time out and our bench erupts. It was at that moment I knew Kiwi was one of the realest I had ever coached. We went on to win that game by 50 points and once that hit the wire we were THE team to come see.

That summer I can recall coach's row being standing room only for our 8 am games. All the major head coaches in the country were lined up early to come see us play. Roy Williams, Billy Donavan, Coach K just to name a few. I met so many coaches that summer and continued to grow my network. It grew exponentially that summer for obvious reasons. It's funny how coaches treat you when you have some of the best players in the country on your AAU team. They will definitely look out for you at that moment. We had coaches asking for Oakland Soldier T-shirts, wearing them to our games, it was bananas. We were the rock stars of the AAU world that summer. Here's a funny story, when we went to Vegas for the Fab 48 tournament all the vans were checked out because I guess we got a late start in reserving vehicles. We ended up having to rent 3 drop top Ford Mustangs for that tournament. It was nothing we had planned but it was very fitting that when you saw these three sports cars pull up back to back, we were the team that was in them.

After having a really great regular season in the EYBL we head to Peach Jam as one of the favorites. We were playing well and thought that we could win it all. We had beaten several of the top teams in the regular season and our confidence was really high. By the time you get to Peach Jam, every team that makes it is really good with a lot of top prospects in the country. We ran through the first three teams pretty easily, and were riding high. Our last match-up in pool play was against a tough team from the DC area, Team Takeover. They were a very talented team that played really hard, and with a different level of hunger than a lot of teams. The way the gym was set up, the players had an entrance in the back in which we had to walk under the court in order to get to the gym. All of the teams had to take the same path to the gym. There was a workout area there where many teams hung out before their games. As we walk through the building we see Team Takeover hanging out, and as we walk through I hear Kiwi saying "we're handing out L's today'. That's why I love this dude. His confidence was always high, and having been an underdog his entire life he had been used to fighting for respect. He wasn't scared of anything, and was up for any challenge. As a coach I loved his confidence, but sometimes it can come back and bite you if you aren't careful. Team Takeover didn't speak with their mouths, but when that ball went up, they commenced to handing us our worst loss of the summer. They played harder and tougher than any team we had faced and jumped on us so quickly; the game was over in the first 5 minutes. At one point, a player on their team scored and ran past our bench and pointed at Kiwi. We took that one on the chin and had to focus on tournament play. We bounced back, but we had a hiccup in our chemistry with a player or two. We ended up making the final 4 and had to face the St. Louis Eagles. This was a very talented team with two of the best wings in the country in Bradley Beal (Washington Wizards) and Ben McClemore (Sacramento Kings). We had beaten them earlier in the summer but Ben didn't play. We knew this was going to be a tough game, and a matchup with many of the best guards in the country playing against one another. They ended up beating us in a tough game, and that was the end of the Nike Circuit.

Although we had our struggles in Georgia, we were still pretty confident going into Vegas. This was the tournament where we had to rent the Mustangs. We were back on our rock star status. This was the first annual Fab 48 tournament in Vegas. This has become one of many big time tournaments that are held in Vegas at summer's end. I don't know what changed but we peaked around this time and things were clicking on all cylinders. We were destroying teams in pool play, and were looking like the best and most exciting team in the country again. Coach's row was still filled with many of the top Head Coaches in the country and we put on a show. We were sponsored by Drew Gooden at the time, and he would come out and watch us every summer. This event is held at the same time that the NBA has their summer league, as well as team USA. Lebron James was in town with team USA and Drew and Mark convinced him to come see us play. We were that exciting and good. Lebron came out and got to sit in an entire section by himself with Drew. We ended up winning the tournament by beating a really good Iowa Barnstormers team, and the game was capped off by a breakaway bang out by Kiwi that set the gym on fire. That was the best we had played all summer, I was even impressed by how well we played.

Prior to the summer starting, Mark and I had decided that if I wanted to get a college job that this would probably be my last summer coaching with the Soldiers. The NCAA had put in this wonderful rule that no one knew the details of called the "Individual Associated With a Prospect" (IAWP) rule. Most people's understanding of the rule was that any AAU coach had to be removed from their AAU organization for a 2 year period in order to be eligible to get a job at a school that was recruiting players from your program. Many people were under the impression that if a school wasn't recruiting any players from your program that it would be ok to hire that coach. Every coach in America was recruiting my kids so it really put me behind the 8 ball. I wasn't able to work camps because of the rule, which really helps build your network with head coaches. Our thinking was this would take me off of the board for 2 years and I would be fine after 2012. As Lee Corso would say, Not so fast my friend. No one had really read the rule in its entirety, and we didn't really have a grasp on how deeply it would affect my life for the next few years. Here is the rule in its entirety:

Bylaw 11.4.2: For a 2-year period before anticipated enrollment and 2-year period after actual enrollment.
No employment in any athletics department noncoaching staff position or in strength and conditioning staff position.
IAWP Definition part 1: Any persons who maintains or directs others to maintain contact with a:
Prospective student Athlete (PSA),
PSA's relatives or legal guardians, or
PSA's coach.
*Contact at any point during basketball participation.

Definition Part 2: Whose contact is directly or indirectly related to the PSA's
Athletic skills and abilities, or
Recruitment by or enrollment at an NCAA institution.

Individual Associated with a PSA (IAWP) could include (but is not limited to):
Parents,
Legal guardians,
Recruiting advisor (Handlers),
Personal trainer, or
Coach.

Pre-existing relationship does not negate IAWP status or make actions permissible.
Pre existing relationship nonfactor in violation analysis.
Pre-existing relationship may be considered mitigation in determining penalties.
Classification and analysis of IAWP is prospect-specific.
Once classified, individuals retain IAWP status during PSA's enrollment
May be considered IAWP for multiple PSAs.

Institutions may be faced with a choice between IAWP and a PSA
What is the result if an institution hires as IAWP and the PSA (with
whom the IAWP is associated) enrolls at the institution within the
prohibited time period?
The PSA would be permanently ineligible at the institution.
The PSA could transfer and be immediately eligible through an SLR
waiver.
  What is the result if an institution hires the IAWP a year later?
The SA would become permanently ineligible at the institution.
SA could transfer and be immediately eligible through an SLR
waiver.
May an institution avoid a violation by moving the IAWP from
a noncoaching position to a coaching position of if the IAWP is
fired?
No. The specific time period continues to apply based on
when IAWP was hired in a noncoaching position.
Does the legislation apply to college coaches?
Yes, Any PSA (including 4-year transfer students) who are
associated with the coach who enroll within the specific time period
would be permanently ineligible.

If you sat there and read all of that and are still as confused as you
were in the beginning, welcome to the world of these coaches and
myself. It's an absolute ridiculous rule and very hard to understand.
I will give you the quick and dirty version, if you coach, or train, or
know a kid who is a prospective student athlete at a particular
school; you cannot be hired in any position other than full time
assistant coach, two years on either side of that player enrolling at
that school. Let me break down why the rule is in place. A few
years prior, a major university hired and AAU coach of the number 1
prospect in the country in order to land that player. They made him
the highest paid assistant coach in the country to basically get that
kid to go to the school for one year. That is why the rule was put in
place, so schools couldn't buy a kid through their handler. I totally
understand the rule and what it was meant for, but it certainly
wasn't meant for guys like me. This was the second and most

pivotal hurdle that was placed in my way on my journey to become a college coach. Beyond that, it would have a major effect on my personal life as well as financially.

For several years I had regularly participated in open gyms held at California Maritime Academy. I had seen the cycle through coaches and be a program that struggled. They had recently hired a head coach that was turning the program around. The summer of 2011 Coach Brian Rooney sat down with me and picked my brain about joining his staff. He and I had a good relationship and he knew my struggles of trying to get into college coaching. I had spoken to him about gaining some college experience. I felt this would be a good opportunity for me to get some valuable experience, work for a coach that I really respected as a person and a coach as well. I was on board, Go Keelhaulers.

Chapter 10: Go KeelHaulers!
"Get better. Every Day"
Bryan Rooney

When I took this job I had no idea what to expect. I played division 1 basketball, I had coached division 1 players for the past several years, and I had dealt with division 1 coaches. California Maritime Academy is a NAIA division 2 school. I had never even watched the team play. Occasionally I would read about them in the Vallejo Times Herald, our local newspaper, and I had played open gym with the guys for the last several years to keep myself in some decent shape. Much to my surprise, I think I liked coaching these kids more than any other level. Never had I seen the pure jubilation in student athletes. These kids were just happy to be playing college basketball. They had no agendas, no one was worried about their numbers or "getting to the league", they played out of sheer enjoyment for the game, and that is why I coach. It was a perfect fit. When I tell you they would run through a wall for Coach Rooney, they would probably attempt to if he'd asked. The buy in was like nothing I had ever seen. Much of it was because they were some awesome young men, but mainly it was because Coach Rooney was the best I have ever seen at getting his players on the same page. It was masterful they way he'd orchestrated the culture there. As coaches, we all want to be able to bring young men from all walks of life and bring them together to achieve one common goal. As cliché as it sounds, that's essentially what we all try to do as coaches. Well, Coach Rooney is the still to this day, the best I have ever seen. His ability to bring the energy every day, in such a positive way and still hold each and every player accountable was amazing to observe. He was firm, but the love over powered the times when he had to bring the hammer on the team, or a player. He was very calculated with his words. He knew exactly how to say things when disciplining a player as to let him know to straighten up and give better effort, but not to affect his confidence. If a kid wasn't playing well he wouldn't tell him that, he would say things like "we need you to play better, you're a key piece to this team, and you've got to play better". Invariably the kid would end up performing better when he returned to the court. Coach Rooney was a tireless worker; honestly I don't know when he slept. I learned from him that you have to out work your team before you can demand that they give it their all. He was always as prepared for his opponent as he could possibly be, and prepared the team in the same way. I don't recall a time where we were caught off guard by anything that an opponent had done.

When Coach took over the program, to say that it was struggling would be an understatement. It is a great school academically, but had never really focused on the athletics. I am not sure how many games it had won the previous years before Coach took over the program but it wasn't very many. Many seasons had ended in 5 wins or less if I am not mistaken. The previous year, which I believe was his second season, he had won the CalPac regular season title and had the CalPac Player of the year. The program was turning the corner in a big way. Our preseason that year was brutal. We had a big win early again Notre Dame De Namur, A NCAA division II school, but went 0 for the month of November following that. Two of our best players were out with injuries, and we struggled to find a point guard. After a discussion between Coach Rooney and the Three assistant coaches, we decided to insert a young man who had been the 12th man at best. He was having some troubles adjusting to the school, as well as him not being the best practice player; he never really instilled the faith in the coaching staff that he could be of much help. Boy were we wrong, this kid would end up being the starting point guard for the next two years, and in his senior year he would lead them to the national tournament in Branson.

We ended up turning our season around and made it to the title game in the conference tournament where we faced Holy Names University. This was a bit of a rivalry. This game was nip and tuck the entire night. They had a heavy set guard who posed some matchup problems for us. He couldn't shoot outside of 3 feet but he was crafty and the coach would run him to the block and post our guards. He liked to stir it up a bit and talk a little trash, which was fine to me, I like when guys talk a little bit. I was never a talker unless guys started talking to me. We ended up taking a 1 point lead with under a minute left, they had the ball, and they isolated the guard and he drove hard baseline from the right wing. Our big, Dave Prindible, a 6'6 leaper came over and got a piece of the initial shot, unlucky for us, he was able to get possession and sneak a layup in to give them a 1 point lead. Our PG came down and got a look at the basket that didn't drop and our season was over. It was a tough pill to swallow but for the most part it was a great experience.

Since then the Keelhaulers, led by Coach Rooney and staff have won the conference tournament 5 years straight and have been ranked in the top 25 nationally. They became the first team from the CalPac to win a game in the national tournament. In 2012 they became the first team to go undefeated in the CalPac. Coach Rooney's resume speaks for itself, but if you haven't been on the journey with him, it's a very different experience to watch this man work. I was so thankful to have had the opportunity to learn from him. I believe that I became a much better coach from this experience and I value that year probably more than any other year of my coaching career. If I can go an entire year and not have 1 player complain about having to run a 17, I will know that I am on my way to Rooney status.

Chapter 11: City Living!

2011 was a very pivotal year for me and some of those around me. Chanee and I had rekindled our relationship and was becoming very serious about one another. I started a job working in San Francisco, which meant I could no longer help out at Maritime. I was pretty much staying in the City with my Great Aunt who lived like 3 minutes from my job. This was good for me because I hate traffic so much, and that commute wasn't something I looked forward to doing daily. This allowed me to stay in the city about three nights per week. This was very bad for my relationship at the time though. Because I had been coaching since I got out of College I had always worked in education where the money isn't great. This job was the first job in which I was making some decent money. This was also the first year in a long time in which I did not coach. I didn't coach any school ball or AAU ball because of the IAWP rule. This would put me at two years removed and I would be eligible again to accept a job at any school. At least that's what I and the people in my circle thought.

Still harvesting my network that I had build up over the years, I booked a trip to Seattle to watch My little brother Desmond Simmons, who played at the University of Washington at the time, and Jabari Brown, who ended up leaving the University of Oregon after the second game of the year. I flew up and rented a car and got a room near campus. While I was there I reached out to An Assistant coach on the Oregon staff that I had become cool with. He invited me to come to the arena to meet the Head Coach. I drove down to the arena and walked in and was able to sit down for about 15 minutes with Coach Altman while the players warmed up for their walk through. To me this was pretty amazing that a coach that I had never met would spend time with me before practice. I mean he sat there with me and had a full on dialogue about his background, how he coached Mitch Richmond, and his journey. He essentially told me that he owed his success to Mitch Richmond. He coached him in Junior College, and then was able to get hired at Kansas State where Mitch attended college and the rest was history. Now let's be clear, Dana Altman is a hell of a coach. He has had great success since he's become a head coach and I think he is one of the most underrated coaches in the NCAA, but what he was telling me was that his big break came because he coached Mitch Richmond. That actually just hit me as I am writing this. But I sat and watched him lead that practice, and very similar to Coach Rooney his energy was infectious. He was ON, and the players fed off of that energy. He was positive, held the guys accountable, but never talked down or yelled in a demeaning manner. He showed a genuine "care" for the players. As I got to know him even better, I can tell he does have a place in his heart for his players, and that isn't something that's universal in that world.

I don't remember who won that game that night, but I believe that Washington may have won. But after our conversation coach Altman said I should come out to Eugene to see that campus. At the time I was spending every dollar I had on getting a college job, so when he said I should come up, I bought a plane ticket to Portland and drove in to Eugene for the next Washington matchup in January. I remember Oregon gave UW the business this time around, but I had a meeting with Coach Altman and they were going to have a graduate assistant position open up. If you are not familiar with what a graduate assistant is, it's basically a grad student assistant coach. I would be working on my masters, from the University of Oregon, and helping out the coaching staff in whatever capacity they needed. This was going to be my IN. This would be a great opportunity to work with a great head coach, who is also well connected, get a master degree which would open up so many doors for me and I would be one step closer to being a college coach. So for the next few months I was riding high. I would of course look for a full time assistant job somewhere if I could but I would have a great situation to fall back on.

I pretty much began the process of transitioning. I told my boss that I would be leaving in August, and Chanee and I had talked about her and the kids moving up to Oregon with me. During this time she had been going through some of the worst times of her life. Me being blind to it all wrapped up in my own stuff I had going on I didn't see her pain. I was working in SF 5 days a week, and I was running my training business that I had started on the weekends. I was training about 50 kids at this point and I was basically working 7 days per week. This put a major strain on my life in many ways. I ran myself into the ground as well as my relationship. Going to Oregon would provide the escape that we both needed. We would start a new life, and I would be pursuing my dreams. Coach Altman is a well respected coach and if I worked hard for him then doors would begin to open and I could possibly become a full-time assistant somewhere. It was an exciting time for the both of us. Until I got a phone call that would truly alter my life in so many ways.

Chapter 12: Individual Associated With a Prospect.

"Life's problems wouldn't be called "hurdles" if there wasn't a way to get over them."
Unknown

A few chapters back I told you all about the infamous IAWP rule. Well that phone call I got from my guy was concerning that rule. The compliance office had informed the coaching staff that it was against NCAA regulations for them to hire me in a "non coaching" position. They seemed to be as shocked as I was. They had signed a kid that I had coached three summers prior to me even meeting Coach Altman and his staff. The two were unrelated but by the letter of the law I could not accept the position at the University of Oregon. Now I have to remind you that, I had left my job, which paid pretty decent, and had pretty much shut down my business. I was devastated. I had no clue how to combat this. I could have asked the school to petition the NCAA but they were already petitioning to clear a player and I didn't feel it would be in good taste to ask them to do that for me. Maybe I should have because the next four years of my life would be me trying to recover from this event. So I spent the next few days scrambling and trying to figure something out. I had a huge going away event that so many people attended and had congratulated me on my accomplishments. This was a pretty big deal for me and I was proud that I had "grinded" hard enough to get this opportunity. Most guys don't get their first gig at a place like Oregon unless you played there. THIS WAS HUGE. And for it to be stripped from me and there was nothing I could do was heart breaking. My girlfriend knew how devastated I was and was there to comfort me but there was nothing she could really do. I was able to get my job back part-time and I started training again to try and keep myself busy, but the whole time I was unknowingly showing signs of depression.

By this time it's almost September, and all the college jobs were dried up, not that I would have gotten one, but I could have at the least expanded my network of coaches. I was pretty much moping my way through life trying to seem un-phased by this ordeal, but I felt the weight. I was living on 60% of what I had been previously making, and I was just not a happy person. All the while my girl friend was going through some of the worst times of her life and we were struggling as a couple. I didn't know how to be there for her, and she was exhausting herself trying to love a broken man. Because of our issues she and I would go through several break-ups and then reconcile only to break up again. Our love for one another was undeniable but our worlds were very different. She was settled and a mother, I was a free spirit chasing my coaching dreams and everything else was secondary to the dream. She was fully in support of my dreams and had my back but I didn't know how to reciprocate the love and it wore on us. We would be happy for a few months and then break up for a few months and then get back together and then break up. Our love was undeniable but we could not make it work.

The next few years were much of the same. Me chasing the coaching dream, going to Final Fours and Pac-12 games and tournaments, training and trying to make things happen. Had I know then what I know now I would have saved a lot of money. You cannot just Bogart your way into the game. It's all about relationships and who you know, and the right person getting the right job at the right school. It's about "having players" for a guy like me. Coaches wouldn't look at a guy like me and think that I could help in the "basketball" aspect of coaching, only getting players and maybe player development, which I learned isn't high on the priority list at the college level either. I would have to be a guy who could deliver players. I always told myself that I would not ride the coat tails of a kid to get a job. I already have an issue with the treatment of athletes at the college level, and I wasn't going to USE a kid. I have learned that this is pretty much the reason that I never got an assistant job but I digress. I don't think the business would find that to be something they'd agree with but I know better. I was almost done trying to get in after exhausting my funds and my spirit, what little I had left. Something inside of me told me to go to the Final Four one last time. Before I went down I had learned the former NBA great Reggie Theus had gotten the job at Cal State Northridge. I didn't know Coach Theus at all but my guy at Oregon had previously worked with him while he was the head Coach at New Mexico State. He made a call and Coach Theus agreed to meet with me. I drive over to his hotel and we grabbed a table and we sat down and chopped it up. I had heard really good things about Coach and he was a super cool dude. We chopped it up, I told him what I was looking for and I had told him about my journey and the whole Oregon thing. He had literally just gotten hired so he was still trying to figure things out with his staff. He did say he was impressed with me and he liked my size and he would see what he could work out. That was promising but I still had to keep hustling. At the time there was a few more jobs open down in So Cal and I was all over them. Upon returning from the Final Four I took a road trip to pop up on the coaches that had just gotten hired or had an opening. The first stop was coach Enfield at USC. I had a guy that had gotten hired there and I hit him up and told him I was in town. Coach Tony Bland was his first hire and he was a guy I went way back to High School with. He was on that Westchester team that beat St. Joes in the state final game our senior year. He was a really cool dude that I had gotten to know pretty well over the past few years. I went over to the school and kicked it with him for a minute and I was able to sit down and speak with Coach Enfield. He had his assistant coaches in place already, and oddly enough USC doesn't have a graduate assistant program. That's kind of where that ended, but he was a great person to talk to and I appreciated his time. Next stop was Loyola Marymount. I had a guy over there that was about to leave and take a job with an NBA team. I knew the position was going to open up I wanted to be ahead of the game. So I drove up to campus and I popped up on coach Max Goode. When I tell you this man would have talked to me until the next day, I mean he would have talked to me until the NEXT DAY. We had a great conversation. To show you how small the basketball world is, coach Good was the head coach at Maine Central Institute in 1998 and coached one of my high school teammates who did a 5th year there. 7 foot Wesley Wilson, who went on to play at Georgetown. He had all of the stories about Wes, and so did I. He was honest and said he had a guy lined up for the position and that if he didn't accept the position then he would call me in for an interview. I appreciated his time and I and felt good that I had gone over there. It's very funny to me that every time I would meet a coach they would tell me how "impressive" I was. I am sure the tailored suits and click clacks helped, but when you prepare for something for so many years, and you know what the hell you're talking about then of course you will be impressive. But I never seemed impressive enough to hire. So after meeting up with coach Goode I sped over to Northridge to meet up with Coach Theus. The whole time I was talking to Coach Theus I was also in communication with Coach Bland's best friend Jay Morris who was an assistant at Northridge. So I stopped by and chopped it up with Jay for a minute. I was able to meet the other two assistants and a few people around the office. When Coach got there we met up and he said he was still working on things to try and get it done. They had never had a graduate assistant at Northridge so they were essentially trying to create one. When I heard this I was even more eager to find a full time position on someone's staff. I really wanted to work with Coach Theus, but I knew this would be a tough gig to take.

So it just so happened that Coach hired a guy from Loyola Marymount which created another opening on Coach Goode's staff. I immediately called Coach Goode and tried to make it happen. He was truthful and told me who he was going to hire and that he appreciated me reaching out. Once again I had pretty much missed out on all of the jobs on the west coast, I also missed an opportunity at Columbia by a few days. I always felt like I was close and "on the verge", but that wasn't good enough. All of the dissapointmentf was building up and I tried to ignore it. But I was almost at my tipping point.

After it was all said and done, I ended up accepting the Grad Assistant position at Northridge because I felt like it was the only way I could get in and also that Coach Theus had enough connections to help me out. Little did I know that the school had infrastructure issues and didn't hold athletics in high esteem? I was walking into a situation that would put me further behind the eight ball financially. Please still remember that I am trying to recover from the Oregon situation from a few years prior. All the while I am thinking about leaving, I never thought about the "family" I was leaving behind. My girlfriend and her children. I had never really thought of us as a family because we had never lived together and I was always so wrapped up in my own life that I hadn't stopped to realize that's what had been formed. I was helping little man with his homework, and helping baby girl learn to read. Going on family movie nights, eating dinner as a family pretty much every night that I could, and I never really paid attention. It was almost scary how easy it was for me to leave. Again, she knew this was something I had to do; she had been there through the many disappointing times and had supported me through them all. I know she hated to see me go. And that last day we spent together was the most bitter sweet moment I have ever experienced. I had another going away event and this one was much bigger. This time I was actually leaving. This time people could truly be proud of me and go on this journey with me. This time I was really leaving Vallejo.

Chapter 12: Go Matadors

One August Evening, I believe it was the 19th; I packed up my car, kissed the kids, kissed their mom and drove off. I can still remember seeing them watch me drive off in my rear view mirror. I stopped off to gas up, grabbed some sunflower seeds, put on the Joe Budden "Mood Muzik" catalog and got on the freeway. Where I was going was a mystery. I hadn't found a place to live, I only had a few friends in LA, and I really didn't know anything. I just knew I was going to join a college basketball staff and that was it. I knew school started on the 23rd and that was about it. This was not a good sign. I was going to be making $1,000 a month and living in So Cal. I was going to be turning 33 in two days and I was going to be making $1,000 per month. WHAT THE HELL WAS I THINKING? Who allowed me to do this? I ended up having to take out a loan for 25K in order to survive. When I tell you that got me to the last day of school, I mean that last dollar was spent on the last day of the school year, HAHA. As I was on my ride, I reached out to the home girl Kourtney who was now living in LA. I also talked to my boy Jay Morris. He told me to hit him when I was pulling into the Valley. That was my first stop. He lived right off campus. I got to his house right before dusk. We sat there and chopped it up, I met his wife and we sat there and he filled me in on the things he thought I should know. He was still kind of figuring things out as well because he had only been working for coach for a short time there. We chopped it up and then I went to Kourtney's crib and crashed there for the night. I had a car full of clothes and no place to live. At most schools when you get a Grad Assistant position they pay for your school, and room and board as well as give you a stipend. That would have been the deal at Oregon. I know the Northridge is not Oregon, but they offered me no assistance in any of these matters. I had to find lodging on my own and I had to pay for my own school. This threw me for a loop. I thought that my schooling was going to be paid for, and had that been the case it would have been an ok situation. The fact that I had to take out that loan would be the reason I would leave at the end of the school year.

College coaching was everything I thought it would be. Although I wasn't full time, got a chance to really experience coaching at that level. I loved it. And working with coach Theus was such a great learning experience for me. Coach loved to talk about basketball and anyone that knows me knows that I can talk about ball until I am blue in the face. To have a chance to work with a 14 year NBA vet and former All-star was truly a blessing. I learned so much about the game from him it's ridiculous. What I learned from Coach Rooney was a lot about work ethic, how to work with your players and some vital basketball information. Coach Theus taught me about basketball on an entirely different level. This man was an offensive genius. I believe that we are very similar in our coaching styles. I am not the "rah rah" guy and neither was he. He was just himself. He got into guys when he needed to but for the most part he was laid back and loved to teach the game. He was very charismatic and very media savvy. He made me think of the game in a totally different way. He taught it from the professional level which I had never been privy to. I learned so much new information and terminology that I didn't know. I love learning about the game and I soaked it up like a sponge. Although that year set me back in many ways, it definitely made me a better coach and I am thankful that I had the experience.

The first month in So Cal was crazy. First of all, I wish someone had told me that the Valley was 100 degrees every day during the summer. I mean this heat was unbearable. I have never experienced anything like it and I went to school in Texas. I spent summers in Houston, and it did not compare to this heat. It was ridiculous. Getting to know the players is always my favorite part of the coaching experience. These kids were a bit different though. There is a big difference between Northern California people and Southern California people. It was very apparent that I would have to get used to these kids. They were all very good dudes, but too laid back for my liking. I need excitement and chatter, and being happy for your brother in battle. None of that existed with these dudes. It's almost like that didn't like one another. We had one dude who showed fire everyday and he was a freshman from Baltimore. He had a hard time adjusting to the climate of the practices as well. After a few weeks of me trying to get these dudes amped up during practice, it became a running joke if I wasn't clapping and hyped the boys would say "c'mon coach, where you at? Let's get hype". I was tired of being the only one bringing the energy and I fell back. I also fell back for another reason. First day of workouts, coach had an NBA training camp style practice for the first 4 days. I am at one end working with the bigs. We were working on swim moves and burying your defender. I was holding the pad and my guy JJ Thomas was coming at me. JJ was an undersized inside player but strong as a bull, from Louisiana. JJ hit the pad and spun, and maybe because he's only 6'5 his elbow cracks me right across my nose. I immediately know it's broken, this being the second time this has happened, and I drop like a ton of bricks. I could feel the blood filling up in my nasal cavity and before you know it my nose is gushing. I headed to the training room and they doctored me up. Then I had to go to the doctor to get it straightened out and what not. I was back at practice the next day like a soldier. But I never held that pad again.

It took me a while to find a place on what I was making. Luckily my guy Jay let me crash at his house pretty much every night. When he would stay in LA I would have to figure things out, I stayed at Kourt's a few times and if she wasn't available I slept in my car and showered at the gym. I finally found a place in Van Nuys, on Sepulveda Blvd. Things were looking up, I received my keys and was on my way back to campus for practice and I got rear ended. I didn't really have any major damage but I definitely didn't have any money to get anything fixed. That first month in LA was a rough one but I was definitely excited to be coaching. It kept me sane because as I look back it was a real grind.

Luckily Kourtney introduced me to her friends Jennifer and Baffo. Jen was a LA transplant from San Antonio, one of a kind personality with no filter. Baffo is a Brooklyn dude through and through. That was my crew when I was down there. Kourt was working for the Grammy's so I got to do some "Hollywood" things, like the pre Grammy show and a few exclusive parties. I am not really that type of dude and I am not start struck, but it was cool to get a chance to hear some of the music and what not. We would hit happy hours when I could get to the city, they were my link to enjoying LA. I knew the Valley was known for an industry that I will not mention, but little did I know that the corner in which my apartment was located was the "stroll". I remember a few nights after I moved in, I came home to find two "women of the night" on my corner. I was in disbelief. Come to find out my neighborhood was notorious for having prostitutes and my street was the main location. They would literally be on the corner when I would get up and go to work in the morning, and they would be there at night when I would come home from work. After a while I got used to it but initially it was a shock. After speaking to a few people from there, they informed me that was the hottest spot in the Valley.

Once the season got under way we went through some issues with the NCAA. A few transfers were petitioning for waivers, both of them having valid health reasons and they were both returning to LA. They NCAA denied both of them while granting some questionable transfers at a few high major schools. That's when I learned that the NCAA does what it wants and the "big fish" play by a different set of rules than the rest of the institutions under the guise of the NCAA. That was the beginning of a really rough season for us because they were two kids that were projected to start. Their impact would have been major. They had both played two years of Big East basketball, and them coming to the Big West would have catapulted us to be favorites to win the league. We had a solid group of kids but our biggest issue was that we had no one who could create their own shot. Our main trio of threats started with Steven Maxwell. A 6'5 post who was one of the freakiest athletes I've see. At 6'5 and ripped, he could bang out from the free throw line. He was all motor and all left hand. You could pretty much pencil in double-double for him every night, but he was limited because he was all left hand and under sized. Our second threat was a 6'6 silky smooth scorer named Stephen Hicks. Hicks was a long wing with sneaky hops and was good at finishing from ten feet and in. His issue was that he had no left hand and teams knew it so at times it was tough for him score. Lastly, a 5'11 all heart guard named Josh Greene. He would want me to say 6 feet but I can't give him that. Josh was an underdog from day one, and made himself into a good basketball player. Josh was the one guy who could create his own shot and that could consistently make a 3. Josh was the only guy that coach let shoot 3's consistently, to the point that we attempted the third least 3 point shots in the country. Josh was a hard worker and a big shot maker. The first week I was on campus, he hit me up for a few workouts because he heard I did skill development. He and I bonded out the gate and we ended up with a really great relationship. He is currently playing overseas, and he still hits me up for workouts. I type them up for him, and send him videos when he wants some new stuff. Those were our main offensive pieces and I watched Coach Theus play chess with these dudes all year long. He found ways to get Max the ball in the short corner and elbows so he could go to his left and use his quickness and athleticism. He found ways to get Hicks the ball in the mid post and in the post so he could use his length to shoot over guys. He found ways to put Josh in pick n roll in transition and found was to get him clean looks from behind the arc. It was amazing to watch. He introduced me to the NBA style of coaching.

In the NBA it's less about scheming and more about getting guys the ball in spots where they can be affective. College is mainly about continuity and repetition. In college you run sets to get a post, layup, or a good look at a jumper. In the NBA you are simply trying to get guys the ball in their sweet spots, so they can beat the defender. It's really about one guy being better than the other. In the NBA you do this mainly because the shot clock doesn't allot for much continuity. By the time you cross half court most times you have 18 seconds to get a shot up. Coaches run sets to get an iso so a guy can make a play. That's pretty much what coach Theus was doing with this team. We didn't run motion, really. He ran mostly NBA sets with NBA motion once the play didn't yield a basket. They plays turned into ball reversal and ball screens mainly, to shrink the defense, kick to guys and drive long close outs. Coach isn't a huge believer in jacking 3's all game. We didn't have the personnel to jack a bunch of jumpers either. We were in the bottom 3 schools in the country in 3 point attempts and makes. Where we made up for this was driving those long close outs. We got to the line a ton. That was our best way of scoring so coach harped on it daily. We led the country in free throw attempts and free throws made. It kept us in games and we ended up scoring a lot more points than we thought we would. Hicks, Max and Josh were all great free throw shooters, and they probably shot 90% of our free throws. I learned a lot from watching Coach manufacture offense from these guys (this is something I will have to do for the next few years with my team).

The season was up and down, we played very inconsistently offensively and defensively we were atrocious. Our guards had a very hard time guarding the ball and navigating screens. Guys wouldn't give up their bodies, we were physical at all and we got pushed around. It was rough early on. Coach wanted us to be a "hit first" team, but we didn't have those types of kids. This opened up my eyes as to why California kids were called soft. I had never really taken that serious because in the Bay we produced some pretty tough kids. Kids in the bay play with grit and toughness. These So Cal kids were a totally different breed. They were "too cool for school" I hated it, the coaches hated it and it was why we were so horrible defensively. Guys would run from charges consistently, wouldn't plug gaps defensively, anything having to do with putting their chest in front of an offensive player was not an option. The entire year we were on the verge of turning the corner, but couldn't quite get to the point where every night we looked like the best version of ourselves. Until the last few games of the regular season.

A huge moment for our team was when we played Santa Barbara at their place. UCSB was in second place behind UC Irvine. Side note. UCI has the tallest player in the world currently name Mamadou Ndaiye; he is 7'5 and almost 300 pounds of proportioned human being. When he shakes your hand, he shakes your arm. Really nice kid though. We had surprised them at their place and gotten a victory, I think this gave us the confidence we needed to believe that we could beat anyone in the league. That game was crazy. It was packed and loud and tight the whole way through. We kept the game close and were within one point and had the ball in the last possession of the game. Josh ends up with the ball in front of our bench and Max sets a step up screen, Josh drives it baseline and hit max with a pocket pass. Going to his left, Max has a great float game, and he caught the pass, exploded off of his right foot and tear drops it right over the front of the rim and we erupt. The bench goes crazy, one of the assistant Coaches grabs coach by his coat, Coach Theus rips away from him and all the buttons on his jacket fly off. We watched it on film afterwards and were in tears laughing because he pointed to the guys to get his buttons. That was the moment I think we knew that we were finally playing up to our potential as a team, and that propelled us into the conference tournament ready to shock the world.

The Honda Center in Los Angeles was where the conference

tournament is held for the Big West Conference. We ended up with a five seed I believe, which was pretty good. We had beaten every team in the league except Cal Poly who was the eighth seed. We were playing our best ball of the year and we were feeling pretty confident. We opened up with Hawaii, who we had had two tough battles with. We end up edging them in a close one. While Cal Poly upset UC Irvine in the first round. Our next round opponent was Long Beach, who we had beaten to finish conference play. We ended up winning another close one, and Cal Poly put a pretty good whooping on UCSB. So here it was, the championship game was probably the two least likely teams, but they were the team that gave us the most trouble. Their record was pretty bad; they played a very ugly and rugged brand of basketball that was tough to deal with. They had some guys that could make shots but were not great offensively. They were the most physical team in the league by far. That year was the year the NCAA cracked down on the physical play and put in those "freedom of movement" rules. They were calling everything that year which is why we would drive to contact. Which is also why we led the country in free throw attempts. Well, come conference tournament time it seemed as if the refs had forgotten about these changes and stopped calling the game the way they'd called it all year and Cal Poly just beat the crap out UCI and UCSB with their physical play. That's what happened to us the previous two times we played them so we made sure to show them these games and emphasize that we had to be prepared to be in a fight. We were game. We battled and controlled the game for the most part. We matched each punch that they threw with a combination of our own. It was similar to Arturo Gotti and Mickey Ward in the center of the ring exchanging blows. It was bloody, it was ugly but we were standing toe to toe and not backing down. Under a minute left in the game, we possessed the ball with a two point lead. The clock ticks down, and we get a shot at the rim, the rebound ricochets and Max save the ball from going out of bounds on our baseline. Josh dives on the ball and covers it with his body, we attempt to call time out, and several players from Poly jump on top of Josh and wrap him up. I look up at the clock sure that we will get this time out and be up 2 with: 33 seconds left on the clock. We were the best free throw shooting team in the country. They will be forced to foul us and the game will essentially be over. We were screaming for a time out, the refs blow their whistles and signal...jump ball. The possession arrow was in their favor. So now we need to get a stop in order to secure our victory and a chance to dance. We discuss whatever we discussed in the huddle. I am pretty sure we went "black" on the perimeter which meant to pretty much switch everything on the perimeter. We come out of the timeout and play ensues, they are very vanilla in what they run, was no magic play that confused us, but somehow we got confused. They had a player drive from the wing, he was contained by the primary defender, but for some reason Hicks turned as it to help and lost sight of his guy. The driving player was able to pitch it back to their guard who was waiting at the top of the key and he launched a 3. That ball seemed to stay in the air for hours, as it made its way towards the rim; it felt like the entire arena was silent. Not a breath was taken in the whole place. Every pair of eyes was watching this ball travel, holding the fate of both teams in its hands. Splash! The ball traveled through the net, their section erupted. We inbound the ball with plenty of time left on the clock, Josh attack up the left side of the floor, Tre ends up with the ball and drives it from the wing, comes to a jump stop in the middle of the key, makes contact with a Poly defender, he falls to the floor, Tre rises and shoots the ball towards the rim, a whistle blows, the shot bounces on the rim, rolls around and drops through the rim. We stand in excitement, believing that we have once again taken the lead. We all glance at the ref, he signals to wipe away the bucket, places his hand behind his head, and calls a charge. The same ref that didn't grant us the time out on the tie up had once again made a call in favor of Poly and essentially sealed our fate. Dashed our hopes of turning an otherwise disappointing season into one that none of us would ever forget. Again, referees have played a pivotal role in changing seasons. This was our opportunity to turn around an otherwise drama filled season and what do they do? They mess it up with ANOTHER horrible offensive foul call. Josh, our lone senior was crushed, as I had been sixteen years ago, sitting on that floor of the Oakland Coliseum. I knew no words could comfort him. I knew this young man would remember this moment for the rest of his life, as I remember the moment the buzzer sounded and ended my high school dreams of winning a state championship. The moment the buzzer sounded at McNeese State that would end my playing career. Another moment that I saw this game cause someone that I loved a great deal of pain. Josh and I were really tight and I admired this young man so much, and in that moment I found myself helpless, unable to provide aid to this young man. The rest of the players would have another year to look forward to. They would have another crack at it. Josh would not. And for his to be stolen away from him by this man dressed in black pants, a striped shirt, and a whistle which had the ability to affect the outcome of a game seemed unfair. It seemed heartless, and the game is just that. Heartless.

Chapter 13: Just hold on I'm coming home.
"The best journey takes you home"
Unknown

After the season I had spent the next few months trying to find an assistant coaching job somewhere. This was my regular routine around the month of March. Gear up for the Final Four, reach out to all my connections, work my network and see if I could land somewhere. This time I had some weight behind me. I had done a year on a D1 staff, coach would make calls on my behalf if I needed him to, and I was feeling pretty confident about things. I also felt like if things didn't work out then I would have to give up on this dream of mine. It would be 8 years of floundering through life, putting things off and basically remaining stagnant in life. This would be the last time I would do this. I was getting too old, I had accrued 25k in student loans, I wasn't about to double that, and Coach understood that. I worked my phone, texting, emailing, calling. Any whisper of a rumor of a job that would be opening up I was on it. Nothing solid happened until I spoke with the Coach at

San Jose State, who I had spoken to when he had first gotten the job. He had two openings but had already offered them to two other guys. One had accepted, but the other was on the fence. He said that he would keep me in mind if the other gentleman did not accept the job. Upon returning from the final four, we were on spring break. I was going home for the week to get things in order in case I had to come back home. Plus I wanted to get away and Chanee and I had once again rekindled our relationship. We had split that December, one of the numerous times that we had done this over a several year span. So I wanted to spend some time with her and the kids and the family. I booked a trip on the Megabus because that all I could afford and I wasn't going to drive up. Right before stepping on the megabus I received a call from the San Jose State Coach. He was asking for a copy of my resume. I had a copy in my phone so I sent it off to him. He set up a meeting with me for that Thursday, this was a Wednesday. He wanted me to meet the rest of the staff; this would pretty much be an interview. I was excited. I felt like this would be my big break. I felt like the Bay area would be an ideal place for me to be hired because of all of my connections and work that I had done with the soldiers. SJSU needed a bay area plug in order to turn the program around. I felt like I could be that person. I boarded that bus with the excitement of a young child on the night of Christmas Eve. All the hard work was finally going to pay off. The funny thing about this whole thing is, every time I would meet with a coach, and they would sit and talk to me, it never failed that they would always say how "impressed" they were with me. This happened to me after almost every conversation I would have with a college coach. What does this mean? Did they not expect me to be "impressive"? Did they not expect for me to be able to talk chalk, philosophy, defense, offense, player development? Did they not expect me to be able to talk...Basketball? I mean, I am a coach. I was a pretty good player. The only reason I was good was because of my basketball acumen. My basketball IQ. I have merely been studying the game since I was in high school, and coaching for over a decade now. Maybe they had perceived me as simply an AAU coach, or a trainer. Maybe they thought I was simply trying to use my "soldier ties" to parlay a job. I am a COACH. This is who I am, what I am, and I believe what I was born to be. I literally just got mad in this instance because I now feel insulted. Do not tell me I am impressive. Expect me to be impressive, and be let down if I am not. I would much rather that than the former. I study this game, I have learned from some great coaches that I have worked with; I played for some damn good coaches, so expect me to be impressive. With that being said, I thought I was finally on my way. I boarded the bus about 10 am in Burbank. Ready for my six hour drive. Along the way I would speak to Chanee, my parents, and Mark. He had spoken to the Coach as well, and was pretty confident that he was going to offer me the job. I am sure the high I felt was similar to that of Jimi Hendrix. The moment in which you reach Nirvana has to feel something like what I was experiencing. To see my hard work pay off, to know the times where I spent my last dollar to attend the Pac-12 tournament in LA, or sleep on a former player's couch at the Final Four in New Orleans because I couldn't afford a hotel room. The nights where I slept in my car or some cheap hotel room on the "Hoe stroll" were worth possibly getting bed bugs. The drives from Houston to New Orleans and back because there were no flights available, after sleeping a night in the airport. The broken nose, the nights waiting on the school to send my check so I could buy groceries. All of the times I had broken up with the woman I loved more than anything chasing this dream. The last image I have of them in my rear view mirror as I drove off, their images getting smaller and smaller until they disappeared. It had finally felt like it was all worth it. Until my phone rang around 1pm that same afternoon.

I looked at my screen with excitement, but there was hesitation, and confusion as to what the phone call could be about. Did he need something else? Did he want to reschedule? I wish it was one of those things. Instead, it was the worst news I could have received at that moment. He called and stated that the gentleman that he had initially offered the job had decided to take it. My heart sunk into the pit of my stomach. It's like all the weight that had been lifted from my shoulders just hours earlier, was now replaced by twice the load. He and I continued to talk and he offered some alternative positions on his staff. I politely declined. I had spent 9 months in LA on $1000 per month; he was offering me similar position with similar pay to live in San Jose. I could no longer take a job making less than $15,000. I felt like all these coaches wanted from me was cheap labor. Now that I had been on the other side and had seen exactly what other coaches were doing, and the money they were making doing it, I would no longer sell myself short. I would no longer be cheap labor for anyone. I knew my value to a staff. I was going to be turning 34 in a few months; it was time for me to move on with my life. I was crushed. I had no time to wallow in the mire; I had to figure things out. I was going to go home. This was the moment I decided to stop chasing a college coaching job. It was like the final punch that would knock me on my back. As I lay, watching the referee count, 1...2...3, I lay, 4...5...6, I lay, 7...8...9...10. It was over.

Chapter 14: What happens to a dream deferred?
"Does it dry up like a raisin in the sun?"
Langston Hughes

I believe "festers like a sore" is the most accurate description of what happens to a dream deferred. It becomes more and more painful over time, it stings, and it becomes infected. Especially when you come so close to achieving them. So I packed up all of my belongings, which fit in the back of a standard flatbed truck, sold some stuff, left some stuff, gave away some stuff, and started from scratch. I didn't even have enough money to rent a truck. I left my car which had blown a gasket, and I was headed home. I asked on Istagram if someone had a truck and was headed to the bay. One of my players felt like taking a road trip and had a truck and he gave me a ride. We packed it up and were on the road. Six hours later I was back in the bay and at a gymnastics recital for Chloe (baby girl). I literally unpacked, dropped my stuff off in my parent's garage, and had them drop me off with the wifey at the gym. I watched in amazement as I had missed months of her development, in gymnastics, and to see her go through this routine brought warmth to my heart that I hadn't felt in a long time. I was home. I was with my family. I felt comfort. This put me at ease for a moment, and shielded me from the fact that I was again slipping into a state of depression.

Prior to me coming home my old boss called me and asked me if I needed a summer gig. I definitely did, so I decided to go back to the city while I was figuring things out. All I know is that now that I had my family back, things would work out. While I was gone, Chanee, my long time off and on girlfriend, had left her job and started her own business. She was a personal chef to some of the Sacramento Kings players, and some local families in Benicia, and Green Valley. Her business was taking off and she was able to leave her day job with Aetna. She had also gone through a transition within herself and was in a great place mentally. I loved watching her blossom like a rosebud; she had become a beautiful flower at the end of a thorn filled stem that had grown from the soil. Her beauty was radiant and contagious. The world around her was filled with rays of light that beamed from off of her face. She was flourishing. Before I came back we had talked about going to Turks and Caicos. I had decided that now was the time to put a ring on it, and Turks was the perfect place. I had it all planned out. I asked her friend to get her ring size for me, and to be discrete about it. She failed. In the midst of her trying to attain the information I needed, she ended up spilling the beans and telling her that I was planning on proposing. Chanee was not ready, and neither was I. She created a rift between us intentionally and we ended up breaking up before She left. Now I had no basketball, and no Chanee. This was always when times were the most difficult. She is my comfort, my main source of happiness, especially when the game would betray me. Without her, and ball the depression was real now. I would wake up and go to work, only to come home and go right to bed. My 2 hour commute from door to door was taking a toll on my mind, and my body. From my car, to the ferry, to the T train, which was an event in itself, every day was taxing. What was I gonna do? I had to have a job. I had bills to pay. I needed to buy a car, I needed to eat, keep my phone on, insurance, and all the other things that cost money on a daily. I was paying almost $300 per month just to commute to and from work. I was hustling backwards and sinking deeper and deeper in my depression, like a lost nomad with his foot stuck in quick sand. I could see myself sinking, but I could not do anything about it, and there was no one around to help me get through this. This lasted a few weeks. Invariably she and I got back together for a few months and for the first time in out 8 years of knowing one another, we spent Christmas together. We rented a room in SF, took the kids to dinner, tried to go ice skating but that didn't work out, and we exchanged gifts and just enjoyed the day as a family. That was a first for me. As long as I had been around the kids, that was the first time I had spent a moment like this where it was just us. It was me, spending time with my family. I keep using the word family because at the time I didn't think about them as my family. It was always Chanee and the kids. It wasn't until our last real break-up that I would learn that this was my family.

I was awakened one morning by a text message. It was late December, a college teammate of mine and really good friend Christian Roa sent me a text reminding me of a game I had told him that I would attend with him. My old teammate Robert who I talked about earlier in the story was now the Grad Assistant at Washington State University where his former coach Ernie Kent had just gotten hired. I had told Christian that I would go with him weeks ago. It just so happened to be on the same day that Chanee, the kids, her friend Liz and her significant other and I were supposed to go Ice skating. I knew this would be an issue. I text Chanee basically trying to do both. Bad idea. She told me to go to the game. She had always come second to basketball, and that was the thing that caused the most friction in our relationship. She was tired of coming in second. I don't blame her for feeling that way. She had watched me get my heart broken, and be constantly disappointed by the game. She had stood by me and supported me in every aspiration that I had ever expressed to her. After all of this time, As much torment as the game had caused me, this would be the last time that she would come second to the game. I went to the game and enjoyed hanging out with my guy Christian. I even joked with him that Chanee may brake up with me over this one. Sadly, I was right. A few days later we had a discussion and she felt like once again I was putting everyone and everything ahead of her. And that was when she told me that, "You should have been with your family". My heart dropped. I had never thought about them in that context. This was the first moment in which I thought I had lost my family. I sunk deeper.

The next few months were spent travelling to and from the City, masking my unhappiness until one day I was having a conversation with my mother and I broke down. The tears just started rolling down my face. I told her I wasn't doing well. She grabbed me, put her arms around me and just held on. I was broken. I had reached my lowest point. I ended up having a conversation with my home girl. We met for lunch one day and we got into a conversation. I told her I wasn't doing well, and she asked me what was wrong. I proceeded to tell her that I needed to get Chanee back and she said something so simple yet so profound, "go get her". I said "how"? I had already tried every trick in the book and had gotten her back too many times. There was nothing left for me to do. She said to me "You haven't done everything yet". I said "trust me, I have done it all." She said, "you need to get a ring". I am sure my eyes almost popped out of my skull when she said it, but honestly that was probably the only way I was going to get her back. I thought about it and in true Damany fashion, I said "why not". The search for the ring began.

Chapter 15: On Bended Knee.

My search began with my home girl; we went to several jewelers, together and alone. She would send me pics of rings that she had found, and I would send her pics of rings I had found. Chanee had sent me a picture of her ideal ring years ago and I had it stored in my old phone. I emailed it to myself on my new phone so that I could reference it when I saw something that was similar. A heart shaped solitaire diamond, with diamonds in the band. Do you know how hard it is to find a heart shaped diamond, but I lucked up and was able to find a ring that I thought she would like, and I bought it.

In the meantime, I had to get out of San Francisco. My boss knew I didn't want to be there and he basically was pushing me out. August 31st would be my last day. We had this discussion in May. He gave me plenty of time to find another gig. I heard about a high school coaching position in Napa, not too far from my home. I had also heard that it was attached to a full time position on campus. I figured I would put in for the job. I knew and athletic director a little bit and figured this would help me get the job. I wasn't excited about coaching, and the program had a rough year the previous year, but I was excited about the opportunity to have my own program. I was more than ready and the fact that I would be on campus would be helpful. So I sent in an application Friday morning, and an hour later I got a call from the AD. He wanted to set up and interview for Monday, but Monday was the one day that I couldn't miss at work. I scheduled it for Tuesday. I KILLED the interview. I had been preparing for this for quite some time, and at my job I taught interviewing skills so I was more than prepared. I did as much research on the school as possible and went in there and knocked it out. I had my second interview that Thursday, and was hired that Friday. Things were looking up.

Chanee and I hadn't talked in months. She had pretty much blocked me from everything aside from emailing. Whenever we would communicate that would be our means. We hadn't communicated for months, and I doubt that she wanted to hear from me. My home girl's suggested that I just pop up. Well that's what I did. We ended up meeting up the next morning before baby girl woke up. I had created a card, and I had my little speech all prepared, but I was as nervous as a canary at a cat show. We sat there on her couch, and I said what I had to say, and I got on one knee, pulled the ring box out of my pocket. She placed her hands over her face and began to shake her head side to side. "No, no, no, don't do this Damany". I was all in. In my mind I knew she would say no because that's my best friend, and I know her better than anyone else in the world. I wanted to let her know that I was serious and that nothing was more important that having her and the kids in my life. The tears poured down her face, as I popped that box open, and that diamond shone her eyes. She continued to shake her head, "do you know how long I have waited for you to do this. This is all I ever wanted from you." Her voice trembling, the tears flowing. I just stared at her, trying not to say much. I just wanted my actions to do the talking for me. We sat, talked, hugged, and even kissed. I think about 2 hours passed and I had to leave before baby girl woke up. She told me that she needed to think about it. She told me that she needed a few days and not to contact her. I understood how heavy this was and I would give her all of the time she needed. She was preparing to go on a trip to Italy and Spain in the next few days. This was hard for me because I knew any time apart wasn't good. I needed time to prove that I was a different dude and that my family was the priority. But it didn't happen, a few days later I was awakened with an email stating that she could not be with me. Too much damage had been done and she felt like none of this was fixable. I wrote my rebuttal, and we went back and forth, and I was able to get her to agree to give it another shot. Again, I felt comfort. I went to see her both days before she left for her trip. Things felt like we were getting back on the same track.

The first few days of her trip we were in constant communication, she was sending me pictures of the coliseum in Rome, their food and all of the wonderful sights they would see. After day three it just stopped. I knew something was wrong. For the next week or so I was awaiting what she would inevitably tell me. She could not be with me. It happened. One night she emailed me and told me to come over early in the morning. The fact that she didn't want Chloe to be around when she told me let me know that once again my heart was about to be broken. I had spent a little time making a welcome home card for her and when I got there I dropped it on her. We spoke briefly about the trip but I could tell by the look in her eye that she was trying to maintain her strength. I have always been her weakness. I had always been able to win her over. I knew my touch would always win in the end. Not today. She looked and me and told me that she could not be with me. That my proposal basically had ruined any chance of us being together. She told me that she knew before she had even left for her trip that we would not be together, but she didn't know how to tell me. She didn't want to hurt me, but there was no way around it. I had already known this day was coming and had been hurting already. My heart beating damn near out of my chest. I cried in her lap as she stroked the back of my head. Comforting me but still holding firm in her conviction to put me in her past. She had tried to do this many of times before, but we had conceited that our love for one another was one of a kind. We were soul mates. We would never love anyone the way we loved one another. Not to say that we would never fall in love with anyone else, but it would never be like this. We were best friends. Our inside jokes with one another. The habits we had picked up from one another like parts of conversations leading us into song. Saying "I ain't got time" when someone would mention doing something that we did not want to participate in. We had become one, our hearts had merged and there was no getting away from this. But at the moment, Damany and Chanee had come to an end.

Chapter 16: Go Braves, Deserve Victory!
"hoping and praying for victory is fine,
but deserving it is really what matters."
Winston Churchill

I started working with the kids at Justin-Siena in June of that summer. I was taking it all in. I was evaluating my talent, and at the same time putting MY stamp, on MY program. I was setting the expectations, creating a new culture, and I had begun the rebuilding process of the program. I was coaching. This is all I had wanted to do for the last eight years. I didn't want to commute for two hours, sit behind a desk, call people on the phone and try to find jobs for people who didn't want a job. I just wanted to coach. That's exactly what I was doing. This would sustain me for a few months. I was finding happiness. A lot of the stress was lifted off of my shoulders. I hired one of my best friends as my assistant. I was back in the game, once again falling in love with the game. Coaching high school returned me to why I fell in love with coaching in the first place. I love teaching the game, and that's exactly what I was doing. I was teaching these young men how to play the game the right way. Many of them hadn't been coached before, and knew very little about the game at its most fundamental level. Like molds of clay, I would be able to shape them to my liking, and in the end hopefully they will be a beautiful work of art. Hopefully they will have the synchronization of an orchestra, every instrument in tune with its partner to the left and right, making the sweet sound of music. Hopefully I can create a team that was beautiful to watch, poetry in motion. Hopefully I could create a team like the ones I'd imagined many nights while staring at my ceiling, hoping for the day that I was on the sideline, suit tailored to structure of my body, my tie dangling down my chest, my arms folded across my chest, as I watch in amazement, My guys, my team, my work of art.

I would be lost in these moments, but when I returned to reality, I was still without the thing that I had come to love most, my family. The smiles of the kids, the touch of my love, the sounds of their voices. I missed it all. As I lay awake at night, my heart would ache, still sinking into depression daily, I would only find solace in the moments where I was doing what I loved, coaching. I finally told some of my friends how I was feeling and they could offer no aid. They would just tell me I would have to move on. I knew this was the answer, but I didn't know how. My heart was with this woman, and I could not pull it from her grasp, and she didn't want it in her possession either. My heart dangled in obscurity, and there was nothing I could do to fix it. So as I sit in this hotel room, peering out the window, having come back from dinner by myself, back to this room, by myself, I will take these next few months to search for my happiness. I feel like this is the greatest journey in life. Happiness to some is the most elusive possession, and some don't even know that they are in search of it.

A few months have passed since the night I sat in that hotel room, feeling a sadness in that moment that stemmed from not spending that evening with the person in which I wanted to. It sparked me to write about this pain that I was feeling. While writing I had the chance to reflect on all of the things that I had gone through because of this game. The pain that I had endured, the sacrifices that I had made only to be let down time and time again. I had in the end made the ultimate sacrifice, I had lost my family. I had decided to focus on my team. I would pour all that I had into them because I felt like because I had made this sacrifice, I had no choice but to spend the majority of my time becoming the best coach that I could possibly be. Not that I wouldn't have otherwise, but there was an underlying incentive. Replacing them would never happen, but I could stop some of the bleeding by submerging myself in this coaching thing so deeply that soon enough the pain would subside and I could live a semi normal life. I had conceded that I probably never love anyone the same way that I had loved Chanee. After having many conversations with friends, they insisted that I focus on myself. Find my own happiness. Work on becoming the best version of myself that I could be. They told me to try and find my own happiness. I kept hearing that old cliché saying "what's meant to be will be". I was beginning to resent these words. I started to evaluate life, and my faith, and all the things I had learned about life from others, and from books. I began forming my own opinion on what life really is. I began to read more, write more, and really try to grow in my craft. I was truly on a path to become a better person. How could I find my own happiness? Be happy? I wasn't dreading my commute anymore. I was working with young people, molding minds and teaching the game of basketball. I was hanging out with friends more than I had been. Although I would still have bouts with moments of depression, mostly at night when I was in bed watching "The Big Bang Theory", things were getting better by the day. I began to take in interest in the history of my people. This was sparked by the recent events that had been going on in the news. All of the senseless killing of black men by law enforcement, and civilians taking the law into their own hands. I wanted to know more about our history, in this country and beyond. I wanted to know more about us then the fact that we were slaves, and the civil rights movement. I wanted to learn about our true origins, the moors, our ancient ancestors. The origin of man. I read a book called "Black Wall Street: From Riot to Renaissance in Tulsa's Historic Greenwood District". The fact that I had never heard about the worst massacre to happen on American soil planted a seed in my heart, and I wanted to water it and nourish it and watch it grow. I read more, "Lies my teacher told me", another book that was very eye opening. I would get lost in these books. This occupied my mind enough to help me grow into a more happy person. Yet still I would have relapses, withdrawals and be thinking of her. I began to play basketball more, submerge myself in the joy that only playing the game could bring.

There is nothing like playing the game of basketball. The bouncing of the ball, the screeching of feet, the voices outside the parameters of the court, these things can only be heard by an onlooker. While you're playing, you can't hear anything except the voice of your teammates and opponents, bodies colliding, and the sound of the ball going through the net. All you can see is the movement of bodies, quick windows of opportunities to score or make a play for a teammate. A screen coming to knock you off of your defensive duties. A shot going up, a quick glance to find someone to box out, only to have to relocate the ball and try and secure a rebound. Or maybe your teammate is coming to set a screen to free you up for a jump shot, you feel your defender on your back side so your set your feet to make a curl and attack the basket. To me, there are few things more beautiful than the game of basketball when it's played at it's most efficient level. I use the word "most efficient", because we look to the NBA as the "highest level" but many times it's not the most efficient. In many instances it's a very bad version of the game that I love. The NBA simply contains some of the best authors/poets in the world. Some of the NBA athletes make the game look so beautiful, most notably Michael Jordan. To watch him was something to behold. The moves he would make, the way he would soar through the air was breathtaking. He had many of the most signature plays in basketball not only because of the huge moments in which they happened (Mike soaring down the lane and switching hands in the finals, or the game winner against Utah) but because of the beauty in which they were made. When these plays are slowed down, they are absolutely enchanting. It's like listening to Marvin's voice over a bed of horns and a smooth baseline, or like Beethoven's 5th for my classical music lovers. It's like hearing Black Thought over a questlove drum solo. Its perfect. This is my ultimate escape from everything. I could be having money issues, my dog could be dying, or I could have had a bad day at work, when I lace up my sneakers and put that ball in my hand, nothing else matters.

After a while I felt like all I was doing was trying to escape though. I was running from the fundamental issue of missing her. Moving on wasn't realistic for me, so I began again to reach out to her, and to my surprise she responded back. We had some dialog about our feelings and to my surprise; she was having some of the same feelings that I was having. She was happy in her life at the moment unlike me, but she expressed that she was missing me too. Over the last 5 years or so we had become more than a couple. We had become best friends. We had become an essential part of one another's lives and this was going to be hard for us to get over. Yet and still, these conversations were brief and mainly ended in her not replying to my last message. I had decided to move on with my life. I would no longer reach out to her. I could no longer subject myself to being rejected by the woman that I loved so much. I never reached out again.

Chapter 17: If you love something let it go...

In the midst of my making one of the toughest decisions that I have
had to make in my young adult life, I felt like I had grown in that
moment. What will be will be, right? I was focused on myself and
my squad. The new job was going well, the kids were working hard.
The Hendrix era had begun at Justin-Siena High School. Within the
first two weeks of me being hired, they local paper had done two
stores on my. I was being recognized in local business by the folks
in Napa. People were excited that I had been hired. Things were
going well. I was getting closer to my goal, happiness. I was
growing as a human being, a coach, a friend and an educator. I was
pushing my guys to become the best players that they could be all
while balancing their outstanding academic achievements. This was
a new journey for me. I was coaching kids who played basketball
for fun. I was used to coaching kids that saw basketball as their
ticket to college. They had put all of their stock in basketball, some
even to the point that they would neglect their grades. That's what
I was used to. I had to adjust my way of thinking. These kids were
planning on attending college on academic accomplishments not
athletics. Some had siblings at Stanford, Davis, and St. Johns. Many
of them wanted to follow in their older siblings footsteps and join
them at these prestigious academic institutions. These kids studied.
All of the kids at the school studied. Many of them were taking SAT
prep courses, and ACT prep courses. Some missing workouts in
order to attend these specialist educators to help them achieve
high scores on these tests. I would have to be ok with this. I am an
educator and I can't expect them to put basketball, which is a small
part of their lives before their academic dreams. That would be
selfish of me. All I asked of them was that they give me maximum
concentration and effort while they are with me. And they did.
These kids worked hard and never complained. They gave me
everything and more each workout. We have created a culture of
them asking for "another one". I stole that from Coach Theus, but

The kids love it. They always ask me for "another one" at the end of my workouts. When finishing up the "4th quarter" in the weight room we normally do a round of four, of three exercises consecutively. We end up doing no less than three extra sets because they always ask, "can I have another one Coach?" I love it. They are hungry. And we eat, eat, eat.

I was in a decent place mentally. I am still close with the people at my old job. They do a yearly retreat in Bodega Bay. Although I was no longer working there, I was still family and still invited. I figured I would go up there and get away for a night before coming back Saturday morning for open gym with the boys. It was a good night. We listened to music, played games, had a good dinner and enjoyed good company. In the midst of us playing our annual game of "spoons", a game similar to musical chairs, played with plastic spoons and playing cards, I got a notification on my phone. An Instagram notification. Someone had liked the picture I had posted of the view from the house that we had rented for the retreat. It was Chanee. This was very peculiar because we hadn't followed one another on social media for years. So I sent her an email. She responded but only once. For the rest of the night I would wonder what that was all about. Feeling of withdrawals had crept back into my heart. My mind locked in on what she could possibly have been thinking when she had liked my picture. Was she just sitting there and missed me, had she double tapped on accident, or was this a message to me that she wanted to reach out to me but couldn't find another way? What do I do with this information? With no answers I simply went to sleep for about 3 hours, woke up and went to the gym to grab a ball, clear my mind, and lead my troops.

That Saturday, she was still heavy on my mind. I decided that I would reach out to her and ask to meet up with her. I sent the email with no expectation, she replied. She had agreed to meet with me for breakfast the next morning. What would I say? How would my words be any different than the previous countless times

that we had sat down and tried to reconcile things? How w
convince her to be with the man that had broken her heart su
times before? How could we repair what to her for so long hau
been not repairable? I wouldn't have to convince her. As we sat at
that table, we had both made the decision that we loved one
another so much and we were not going to be without one another
from that day forward that the words were spoken but
unnecessary. I spoke of starting over, and working on becoming
best friends again, she nodded. I spoke of starting slowly and
building a solid foundation, she nodded. I spoke of wanting to focus
on the reasons that we had fallen in love with one another in the
first place, she nodded. This woman had already made it up in her
mind that we would be together, and that we would be happy, and
I had made that same decision the moment that she doubled
tapped that picture on her iPhone. That "like" led to love. That
"Like" led to two hearts that had found each other one night
in Applebee's almost 9 years prior, merging into one. That "Like", is
the reason I smile today, and have only had happy days since. That
"Like" made it possible for me to have the family that I love so
much, and the game that I love to teach, coexist. The culmination
of all of this will happen the first night that I see my family in the
stands, while I am roaming the sideline, suit tailored to fit,
tie draped down my chest, my arms crossed over my chest,
beaming intensely at five young men, moving with the
synchronization of an orchestra playing Beethoven's 5th symphony.
Flowing together like Marvin's voice over a bed of horns, or best of
all, a cold Black Thought verse over Quest love on the drums.
Although you have hurt me dearly, I will always love you.

Peace and Blessings!

Made in the USA
Charleston, SC
26 April 2016